EVOLUTION OF FUTURES TRADING

Trading Floor of the Chicago Mercantile Exchange

EVOLUTION OF FUTURES TRADING

by

Harold S. Irwin

First Edition

Mimir Publishers, Inc.
Madison, Wisconsin
1954

Printed in the U. S. A. by
WORZALLA PUBLISHING CO.
Stevens Point, Wisconsin

FOREWORD

Futures Trading in agricultural commodities is a major factor in the marketing of these products and yet it is the least understood and often the most condemned part of the entire marketing system. Many farmers and farm leaders have felt that this speculation in their products was not in the interest of agriculture because they erroneously regarded it as a form of gambling; legislators have often maligned the subject of Exchanges in their topics of discussion at farm meetings. The strange part is that very few of our Agricultural Colleges have attempted to give their students any thorough understanding of the principles underlying Futures Trading. For many years an effort has been made to have real basic studies made of Futures Trading in the different commodities, but neither the United States Department of Agriculture nor the Colleges, excepting a few, have appeared much interested in these studies. It is, therefore, a real pleasure to find such a fine and unbiased work on the subject as Mr. Irwin has given in this monograph. His research report does not claim to be any complete study of Futures Trading. It may be the means, however, of interesting other men in the subject and eventually there may be made available through their labors a large source of material on Futures Trading and the activities corollary to this form of exchange.

Hendersonville, N. C., Lloyd S. Tenny

September 15, 1953.

PREFACE

The principal reason for undertaking this study early in 1942 was the opportunity to obtain the help of the older wholesale butter and egg dealers at Chicago in preparing an account of the development of butter and egg futures. A number of those dealers had been in that business for some time before organized trading in butter and egg futures began in 1919. Studies of grain and cotton futures had shown that the published records lacked much of the information essential to an adequate analysis of the reasons back of the development of each; information which presumably could have been obtained earlier from the grain and cotton merchants and brokers. Since such information concerning grain and cotton futures had been lost, there was all the more need to obtain it for butter and egg futures.

Recognition of the pattern of evolution in butter and egg futures led to a detailed analysis of the origin and development of time contracts in grain at Chicago, prior to organized trading in grain futures. This study was followed by a less detailed study of the subsequent development of grain futures and of the development of cotton futures. Because much of the material concerning grain and cotton futures was obtained from secondary sources, this material is placed in an appendix.

Only the surface of the development of grain futures after approximately 1860 and of the development of cotton futures could be touched. It is hoped that this account will stimulate additional research in these fields. Problems of unusual interest include the effects of the growth of both cotton and grain markets in size and complexity upon the development of their futures markets and the reciprocal influence of the futures markets upon the respective commodity markets.

Further analysis also is needed concerning the relationship between butter and egg futures and the marketing of butter and eggs. Futures trading definitely contributed to the substantial reduction in storage margins for butter and eggs between approximately 1925 and 1939 but so did other factors. An appraisal of how much of the reduction is attributable to futures trading and how much to reduced seasonality of production, changes in the organization of butter and egg marketing, or other factors fell outside the limits of the present study.

My debt to many of the Chicago butter and egg dealers for information and to numerous students of butter and egg marketing for helpful comments is great. Especial acknowledgement is due to the late W. S. Moore who was the leader of the group that set up organized trading in butter and egg futures and who was generous in providing needed information. Frequently the writer was told upon inquiry from other dealers as to some specific point, "Oh, I don't know much about that. You go ask Billy Moore. He'll know". Acknowledgement is made also to Mr. Paul Mandeville for access to his unique file of The Egg Reporter and for helpful comments and to Frank E. Pilley, Jr. for making available the early records of the Hanford Produce Company.

Epping Forest,
Maryland,
Sept. 1, 1953.

Harold S. Irwin

TABLE OF CONTENTS

APPENDIX I

APPENDIX II

ILLUSTRATIONS

EVOLUTION OF FUTURES TRADING

EVOLUTION OF FUTURES TRADING

ORGANIZED TRADING IN FUTURES

Its Background and Evolution

In spite of the widespread interest in organized trading in commodity futures, very little information is readily available concerning its origins, its development, and the public purpose which it serves. Lack of such information has permitted the rise of unrealistic notions concerning this trading which tend to distract popular attention from the services which it renders in the marketing of the commodities traded and to increase the difficulties of devising workable means of improving those services.

This volume presents a detailed account of the evolution of futures in eggs from the time contracts beginning about 1890 to the comparative maturity of butter and egg futures at the outbreak of World War II. It presents also a detailed account of the time contracts in grain at Chicago and less detailed information as to their subsequent development and the development of cotton futures.

Information obtained from the older wholesale butter and egg dealers at Chicago who had been in business there long before the beginning of organized trading in futures in 1919 was of great value in analyzing the early development of butter and egg futures. It aided in understanding the customary business practices of various periods, the reasons for the changes in such practices, and the results of the changes. This information had its disadvantages; frequently dealers' memories were vague as to specific items, such as dates. In contrast, the published material was definite as to dates and events but generally lacked information bearing upon day-to-day business practices and the reasons for the changes made. Information obtained from each source complemented that of the other; in fact, information brought together from published sources aided in refreshing dealers' memories upon specific details.

Some bias, conscious or unconscious, may have been present both in the statements of the dealers and in the published material. Some of the dealers interviewed may have wished to present certain events in a favorable light. Some of the articles published in trade journals were prepared in support of the writers' positions, reporters' articles sometimes probably were colored by the attitudes of the persons providing the information, and even some editorials may have been influenced by trade leaders. Efforts were made to minimize the effects of bias by cross-checking the information.

Analysis revealed that the development of butter and egg futures was practically independent of grain or cotton futures. Even when committees of butter and egg men studied grain and cotton futures in 1919, preparatory to setting up organized trading in butter and egg futures, there was no indication that they realized that grain and cotton futures had passed through a similar stage nearly half a century earlier.

The pattern of development of butter and egg futures revealed by the analysis led to a study of the origin and early development of grain futures at Chicago. Here the pattern was very much like that of butter and eggs and the evidence did not support the account given in Taylor's History of the Board of Trade.

More general information, largely from secondary sources, indicated that the development of time contracts in cotton was very like that in grain and in butter and eggs and that after organized trading had been begun its development was generally similar in each of these commodities.

In each instance analysis shows that futures trading, unorganized and organized, developed gradually, evidently to meet specific marketing needs. In eggs and butter such needs clearly arose from the added problems which resulted from the accumulation of seasonal surpluses by dealers. In cotton and grain the same conclusion seems to be warranted although the evidence is less complete. In each instance the time contracts which preceded organized trading arose in response to marketing needs, developed over a period of years as the commodity market grew in size and complexity, and ripened into organized trading in futures. In each instance the organized trading then showed considerable evolution before reaching its full stature. This information should contribute to an improved understanding of organized trading in commodity futures and the marketing services which it renders and should aid in improving the efficiency of those services.

Trading In Chicago Butter And Egg Futures

To understand the developments in butter and egg futures it is necessary to review the beginnings of butter and egg marketing in the Middle West and to outline the changes in marketing conditions as they bore upon the rise and development of time contracts.

Because of limitations of time and space, the outline of early developments will be restricted, in the main, to the marketing of eggs. So far as influence upon the rise of futures trading is concerned, the developments in butter marketing were generally similar but the timing was different. Furthermore, the story of butter marketing is complicated by the transition from storage by commission merchants to outright purchase by butter dealers and by the shift from farm butter to centralizer creamery butter. The story of early developments in egg marketing is simpler and, in general, it provides an adequate basis for an understanding of the development of futures trading in both commodities.

Growth Of Egg Market In Middle West

Back of the marketing of eggs in the Middle West was the growth of the supply of eggs in that region. As the successive areas were settled most farms had some hens, primarily to supply eggs and chickens for the family table. Housing conditions and feeding practices generally were primitive. Egg production was highly seasonal with a heavy lay of eggs in the spring but with hardly any eggs in the winter.

Mongrel Farm Flocks Were Common

Egg production in the Middle West increased especially rapidly after the Civil War. Large numbers of settlers poured into new areas to take up land under the Homestead Act and the extension of railroads facilitated the marketing of the products of their farms. By the census of 1880, the first to include data of poultry and eggs, the Middle Western States had become the largest producers of poultry and eggs in the United States. (70)

As settlement proceeded, most farms produced a surplus of eggs in the flush season. Money was generally scarce and most farm women were eager to trade eggs at the local stores for current necessities. Prices of eggs ordinarily were very low in the flush seasons. One informant mentioned that about 75 years ago eggs in his neighborhood in Iowa might bring 5¢ a dozen in trade but that sometimes there was no market for them at any price. Even as late as 1896 some egg packers in Iowa and Missouri were paying 5¢ a dozen for eggs about the middle of May. (41) Obviously, the surplus eggs in neighborhoods remote from town had almost no value at such times between the infrequent trips to town.

On the demand side, dealers in consuming areas were reaching out for supplies of eggs. The rise of cities and of mining and logging communities, together with some export trade, provided rapidly expanding markets for the increasing quantities of eggs. As production expanded westward the area of the egg market increased by leaps and bounds, and efforts were made to develop channels by which the eggs could move from producers to consumers. As far back as the Civil War a few eggs were shipped to New York from States as far west as Illinois and Minnesota and by 1874 New York was drawing eggs from the central tier of States west of the Mississippi. (70) Doubtless some of the shipments were experimental but a beginning had been made.

Country Marketing Practices Were Crude

Little attention was given to the quality of most of the eggs marketed. In general the eggs were traded at the country stores, although a few farmers shipped their eggs to terminal markets. The stores commonly handled the eggs merely to accomodate their farm customers in order to retain their trade. Frequently the stores made little or no profit on the eggs handled, looking to the sale of goods for their profits. (69) Thus the storekeeper was unlikely to be critical of the quality of the eggs brought in by a farm woman whose family bought large quantities of groceries, dry goods, and other articles.

Bringing in Eggs from the Country

The tendency was for the stores to ship out the eggs with a minimum of attention. Frequently the attitude was "An egg's an egg as long as it has a shell". Little attention was given to the need for increased care to maintain quality as the widened market increased the average time between production and consumption.

At first most of the stores which accepted eggs in excess of local requirements were within moderate distances of such terminal markets as Chicago and St. Louis and could ship the eggs conveniently to commission merchants in those markets. A few enterprising storekeepers had connections in eastern markets

Country Stores Gave Eggs Little Attention

and shipped eggs there. As the egg-producing areas extended westward, the storekeepers in the more distant localities tended to ship more to the newer and smaller markets, such as Omaha and Kansas City.

Interior Packers Contributed To Improvement

As population became denser and egg production increased, and as the railroad net tapped new areas, egg packers and shippers began to appear in the interior cities of the Middle West. In Iowa, for example, such shippers may have become established in Burlington and Dubuque before the Civil War. Later, egg shippers appeared at Waterloo, Ft. Dodge, and Sioux City, to name only a few places, and still later other shippers established themselves in a number of smaller cities. In much the same way carlot shippers of eggs arose elsewhere in the Middle West wherever adequate supplies of eggs could be obtained.[1]

Many of these shippers began in a small way. Some may have begun with the shipment of comparatively few cases, perhaps during the flush season only. Presently a number of them became well established and built up substantial businesses. In addition to assembling and shipping eggs, some of them came to place substantial quantities of eggs under refrigeration.

The rise of interior egg packers and shippers brought improved merchandising methods closer to the producers than when the eggs had been shipped to the terminal markets. In contrast to the country storekeepers, the egg packers and shippers generally were experienced in egg merchandising. While some of the smaller ones shipped their eggs to nearby markets, some of the larger interior shippers established connections with dealers in Eastern cities, principally in New York, and competed with Chicago egg forwarders.[2] Some interior shippers also had connections in the South and a few also shipped eggs to the Pacific Coast and the Rocky Mountain points. One observer estimates that perhaps only 10 percent of the eggs handled by interior shippers in the decade preceding World War I was sent to Chicago.

The interior shipper enjoyed several advantages. He could adjust misunderstandings with country stores to better advantage than could terminal dealers because he was closer to them. He could check deterioration earlier because he got possession of the eggs with less delay than the more distant dealers. This was especially important in very hot or very cold weather.

[1] Frequently the opening of a plant or a buying station which paid cash for eggs aroused considerable interest among nearby farmers. It was likely to stimulate local egg production, particularly in a time of depression.

[2] In 1895 the Chicago dealers were jubilant because the carlot rates which the interior shippers had enjoyed were abolished by the railroads. (23)

A further advantage was in his cost of transportation since the eggs sent to him moved only relatively short distances at less than carlot rates.

At the outset many of the interior egg shippers may have shipped their eggs as received, but soon the more alert shippers came to grade their eggs and to put out relatively uniform packs. No doubt the grading was crude according to present standards, but it was an advance over previous conditions. A number of the interior shippers came to be well known in the trade for uniform packs which moved more readily than unknown brands. Such brands either would command premiums or would move at current prices when other packs would not. (See 57)

State Associations Arose

By 1895 numerous interior egg shippers were established in the Middle West. There were enough of them to occasion the publication of a trade journal, "The Egg Reporter", which was begun at Waterloo, Iowa. Approximately at this time, also, a number of State associations of shippers of eggs and butter were organized.

The first such association, the Iowa Wholesale Butter and Egg Association, was organized in Iowa in 1894. (37) Monthly meetings were held, usually at Des Moines, for discussion of the problems of butter and egg shippers. Prominent among the problems were those of freight classifications, freight rates, and grading practices. Prior to the opening of a new egg season an important subject was the price which should be paid for the eggs to be placed under refrigeration. The shippers present did not establish a price for eggs but they discussed the prospects for the coming season and might conclude that prices higher than a given level would be unreasonable.

Within a few years a number of other State groups were organized, including those of Missouri, Indiana, and Ohio. A considerable number of the leading egg men from Chicago and important eastern markets attended the meetings which occurred immediately before the opening of the egg season in order to renew acquaintance with the shippers. The dates of the various meetings were scheduled so that the visitors could "make the circuit".

Chicago Egg Market Showed Rapid Gains

The wholesale egg market at Chicago increased rapidly in size and complexity with the expansion of egg production in the areas tributary to Chicago. Production was mounting so rapidly in the latter half of the nineteenth century that receipts at Chicago increased by leaps and bounds even though interior egg shippers and others sent most of their eggs to other markets. At an early date Chicago became a forwarding market for eggs since the eggs poured into it were in excess of local requirements.

The growth of Chicago as an egg market was favored by its position between the surplus egg-producing areas of the Middle West and the consuming areas of the East. Another factor was the importance of Chicago as a railroad center. Most of the railroads tapping the egg-producing areas of the Middle West had their eastern terminal at Chicago where they made connections with the railroads serving the East and the South. A third factor was the establishment of less-than-carlot refrigerator service west of Chicago by the railroads in the 1880s. This service facilitated shipment to Chicago by many country stores. If a store had 100 cases or more to ship it could usually arrange to have a car set on a siding for loading; a store having a smaller quantity could arrange to have its eggs teamed to a car in a specified train while the train was switching at that station.

The advantages of Chicago's position increased as the storage of eggs in local icehouses gave way to commercial cold storage in large central warehouses at terminals. Egg dealers who formerly had stored some eggs locally came to ship eggs to Chicago for storage and even more of the eastern dealers found it advantageous to place some of their accumulations under refrigeration at Chicago because with the development of "storage in transit" privileges the refrigerated eggs stored at Chicago could be shipped to wherever the demand should become most active. Likewise, the Chicago brokers and dealers were in a position to keep closely in touch with the demand for refrigerated eggs everywhere, particularly in the consuming areas of the East and the Southeast.

The increase in the volume of eggs handled at Chicago may be inferred from annual data of receipts. The available figures include the cars which were shipped through Chicago on their way to New York and other markets but they are the only figures obtainable for the earlier years, beginning with 1889. The data of annual receipts, taken at intervals of five years, are:

Year	Thousand Cases	Year	Thousand Cases
1889	1,018	1919	5,963
1894	2,097	1924	7,469
1899	2,096	1929	6,973
1904	3,114	1934	7,364
1909	4,558	1939	8,090
1914	4,565		

On the whole, the increases were rapid through 1924 although there was some irregularity from year to year. Very likely the proportionate increases were even greater in the years before 1889.

Trade Organization Was Formed In 1874

The first trade organization at Chicago in which butter and eggs were prominent was the Chicago Produce Exchange which was organized on May 20, 1874. Its members included dealers in produce of various kinds, including a few oleomargarine manufacturers. It opened a hall on the northeast corner of Clark and Lake on June 2, 1874, announcing, among other things, that "Heretofore there has been no regular and recognized market in the West for butter, cheese, eggs, poultry, et cetera . . .". It was hoped that the Exchange would attract a number of eastern and southern buyers. (30)

Soon after its formation it had a membership of more than 300. Little is known of its early activities although it was reported to be helpful to the trade in the compilation of trade statistics and in other ways. Interest in it fell off and the Exchange became inactive about 1878. (67) Four years later it was revived and by 1885 it was established in modest quarters at the corner of Clark and South Water Streets. (68)

Presently the butter and egg dealers formed a group within the Exchange, largely because of dissatisfaction with the market quotations on butter and eggs. The wholesale quotations on these commodities had been obtained by the Secretary of the Exchange through inquiry from certain commission merchants as to ruling prices. At a meeting of butter and egg dealers in May, 1894 it was decided to have the wholesale quotations on butter and eggs prepared by a committee of 15. This was done for several days; then on May 26 the committee invited all the wholesale butter and egg dealers in Chicago to join in its daily sessions. The question of egg classification was raised and was settled in June ". . . to the general satisfaction of members of the trade. . ." (24)

On November 9, 1895 the Produce Exchange Butter and Egg Board was organized as a group within the Chicago Produce Exchange. The object of the new organization was to "establish official quotations for butter and eggs in this market. . ." (30)

A few years later dissention arose in the Chicago Produce Exchange over efforts to obtain Illinois legislation to control the sale of oleomargarine. Butter dealers wanted to use the Exchange in promoting such legislation but this was opposed by the members who were manufacturers of oleomargarine. As a result of the dissention the butter and egg dealers withdrew from the Chicago Produce Exchange and formed the Chicago Butter and Egg Board on February 8, 1898.

The objects of the Board were listed as follows:

> "The purposes for which this corporation is formed are to establish for the benefit of its members daily market quotations on butter, eggs, and other products and to furnish general information to its members regarding the market for such commodities, and to furnish a convenient place where its members may buy and sell such commodities, and to facilitate the speedy adjustment of business disputes among its members, and to secure to its members the benefits of cooperation in the furtherance of their legitimate pursuits." (63)

No account of the operations of the Board in its early years is at hand but evidently new conditions called forth new functions. The determination of official quotations was abandoned about 1914 but in the meantime other activities had been undertaken. Describing the Board about 1917, Nourse said:

> "This organization maintains permanent quarters at the corner of Lake and La Salle Streets, where the members meet each morning at nine o'clock for the transaction of business. Wholesale receivers offer such goods as they have for sale, and jobbers and buying brokers make such bids as they think are justified by the conditions and prospects of the market. It is the purpose of the Board to bring the forces of both the supply and demand side of the market together at this daily session (known as the call) so that a rational basis for price making can be arrived at. Only a comparatively few transactions take place at the meeting of the Board and occasionally the bids and the

The Trading Floor of the Old Butter and Egg Board, the Forerunner of the Present Mercantile Exchange

> offers there may represent ideas of value too far apart to be reconciled and the session may close without any sale being effected. Until about 3 years ago, a quotations committee of the Board issued each day a set of official price quotations, but the Government brought suit under the Sherman Act and the practice was abandoned. The Board is still free to meet for the transaction of its buying and selling business and the discussion of trade conditions." (59)

Other functions of the board included the development of grades of butter and eggs and the establishment of regulations governing trade practices. The rules of the Board in 1915 included 63 rules dealing with eggs and 38 with butter. Transactions in both butter and eggs on the spot calls were governed by a number of rules designed to expedite the trading. The Board also operated an inspection service and provided for the arbitration of disputes among its members.

With respect to grades, eggs were divided into "Fresh Gathered", "Storage Packed", and Refrigerator Eggs, with various grades under each class. Under Refrigerator Eggs, there were:

Refrigerator Extras
Refrigerator Firsts
Refrigerator Ordinary Firsts
Refrigerator No. 1 Dirty Egg
Refrigerator No. 2 Dirty Egg

Many important developments have been omitted, perforce, from this brief outline of the rise of egg marketing in the Middle West. To cite one item only, nothing is said of the transition of the sale of eggs at terminal markets from a commission basis to outright purchase by receivers.

As part of the background of organized trading in egg futures, however, it should be emphasized further that the egg market increased rapidly in size and complexity, year after year. Consequently, new problems kept confronting the egg trade and measures which promised reasonably satisfactory solutions at a given time frequently fell far short of trade needs a few years later.

Cold Storage Caused Great Changes In Egg Marketing

Before eggs were placed under refrigeration the egg market was comparatively simple although it was highly seasonal. In the spring when production was heavy the primary objective was to move the supply promptly into consuming channels. During the hot weather eggs from a distance were unsatisfactory. In the late fall some eggs were held back by farmers and by merchants in the hope of higher prices but usually the quality of such eggs deteriorated rapidly. During the winter few eggs were available.

Various attempts were made, of course, to preserve eggs for winter use. Some were packed in salt, some in lime, and some were placed in tanks containing various pickling solutions. Limed and pickled eggs persisted for some time after the rise of refrigerated eggs, limed eggs being quoted on the New York market nearly to the close of the century. Of course the eggs so treated tasted strongly of the preservative and were quoted at substantial discounts under fresh eggs.

Evidently the first attempts at refrigeration of eggs were of eggs placed in icehouses in the fall in order to carry them forward into the winter. Some of the egg men thought that the icehouses had been erected for the storage of fruit and their early use for eggs was incidental. Eggs stored near lemons, for example, acquired a lemon flavor. The first icehouse in Chicago was erected before 1871 (perhaps in 1868) but no wholesale quotations for icehouse eggs at Chicago were found until November, 1877. At that time they were only slightly higher than the quotations for pickled eggs but soon the spread widened. (31)

Comparative quotations at Chicago for fresh eggs, icehouse eggs, and pickled eggs about mid-winter were:

	Dec. 30, 1878 (26)	Dec. 17, 1879 (27)	Jan. 6, 1881 (28)
	Cents per dozen		
Fresh	20	20-21	29-30
Icehouse	14-18	12-18	27-30
Pickled	5-12	Unsaleable	15-25

These comparisons need to be qualified. Very likely some of the so-called fresh eggs were merely eggs which had been carried forward since fall without refrigeration. It is probable that the icehouse eggs quoted were fall eggs. A little later they were quoted at materially higher prices than the eggs placed in icehouses in the spring and thus stored for longer periods.[3]

Efforts were being made also to refrigerate the eggs from the heavy spring lay but many experiments were required and many losses were suffered before an acceptable product could be assured. Largely by trial and error, it appears, workable techniques were evolved and increasing quantities of eggs were placed under refrigeration in the spring months. By April, 1884 a demand for eggs to be placed in icehouses was noted at Chicago with the comment that the grading was strict. (29)

The storage of eggs in icehouses was widely scattered over the more northerly States of the Midwest where ice could be cut conveniently. Numerous egg packers and shippers erected icehouses and engaged extensively in the refrigeration of eggs.[4] Systems of ventilation with blowers and fans were devised which aided materially in turning out a merchantable quality of re-

[3] In New York it appears that the placing of eggs in icehouses began materially later than in Chicago and was done in order to improve the quality of summer eggs. It is reported that the first New York dealer to place eggs in an icehouse, about 1889, put in eggs in April in order to have a supply of good quality eggs in July. (52)

[4] See App. II for some indication of the number engaged in storing eggs in 1896. Presumably the number had been greater a few years earlier but miscellaneous small lots of refrigerated eggs had become hard to sell.

frigerated eggs. Doubtless there were wide variations in the quality of the eggs stored by the various shippers.

Shortly before the turn of the century the development of mechanical cold storage largely supplanted the use of icehouses in the refrigeration of shell eggs. Mechanical refrigeration had come into use for many other commodities shortly before 1890. (7) (33) It was less successful at first, however, with eggs than with most other commodities until arrangements were made for the control of both humidity and temperature.

Much Of Seasonal Surplus Was Stored

The quantities of eggs withdrawn from immediate consumption during the season of flush production and placed under refrigeration increased rapidly during the 1890s and continued to increase during the first two decades of the present century. Presumably the proportions of flush production placed under refrigeration likewise showed increases but no data of the quantities stored were compiled until 1896 (see App. II) and such stocks probably were incomplete. By 1920 a large proportion of the eggs marketed in the spring was refrigerated. Taking an average of the three years 1919-21, the stocks of shell eggs under refrigeration on June 1 at Chicago, New York, Philadelphia, and Boston, combined, equaled more than 45 percent of the arrivals of eggs at those markets during March, April, and May.

The proportion of the spring production of eggs that was placed under refrigeration reached its peak in 1922. In recent years the proportion has decreased, both because of reduced seasonality of production and because of the substitution of frozen eggs for shell eggs by bakers and some other users.

Since substantial quantities of eggs are produced in each month of the year, the proportion of the annual production withdrawn from immediate consumption is much smaller than in the case of an annual crop. Practically all the seasonal surplus of eggs, however, is carried forward by dealers in contrast to the situation in other commodities where a considerable proportion is carried forward by farmers, especially early in the crop year.

"Accumulation" Added A Dimension To Egg Marketing

The building up of inventories by dealers during the periods when farm marketings are in excess of immediate consuming needs and the subsequent withdrawals from inventories to supplement the reduced quantities available during other periods of the marketing year may be termed accumulation. By means of accumulation the dealers involved adjust seasonal production to consuming demand and reduce seasonal price variations.

The decision of an egg dealer to accumulate a quantity of eggs gave rise to inter-related problems of storing, financing, and risk assuming which differed greatly from such problems prior to accumulation. Likewise, the problems of price-determining became more complex under accumulation. These added problems resulted in a more complicated market structure than the former structure of the egg market. In addition, the accumulation of eggs lengthened the egg marketing season materially, making refrigerated eggs available to consumers at times when supplies otherwise would be small.

The principal questions concerning the accumulation of eggs were (1) how many eggs to withdraw from immediate consumption during the period of heavy production and (2) how high to bid prices over the demand for immediate consumption. Later in the marketing year other questions arose, including how rapidly to withdraw stocks from inventories and how high to set the prices of refrigerated eggs. If prices were bid too high during the flush period and too many eggs were withdrawn from immediate consumption at that time, consumers would refuse to purchase the refrigerated eggs at remunerative prices and the dealers would lose money. If the dealers held back during the flush period and placed fewer eggs under refrigeration than consumers subsequently desired, they missed an opportunity for additional profit and risked the loss of customers to other dealers who had refrigerated eggs for sale. Dealers, as a whole, developed considerable skill in judging how many eggs to withdraw from immediate consumption, the maximum prices which they could pay, and the rate of withdrawals of eggs from inventories.

Certainly, society did not consciously entrust to the egg dealers the responsibility of adjusting seasonal egg production and prices to the pattern of consumers requirements. Nor is it likely that the early accumulators of eggs envisaged so far-reaching a result. Yet, as consumers voted in the markets with their dollars for their preferences in seasonal patterns of egg supplies, it became apparent that profits in egg storage deals depended to a large degree upon ability to forecast consumer requirements correctly.

Before accumulation the service of storage in egg marketing had been limited to the incidental storage required in the assembly and the distribution of the eggs. Under accumulation the importance of storage showed a sharp increase since a large quantity of eggs was held for several months under rigidly controlled conditions. Some of the eggs, it is true, might be stored for only a month or two but some might be held from March to the following January.

Financing likewise showed a sharp increase in importance under accumulation. Some money was required to finance the successive shipment of eggs from producers to consumers but the period of ownership of each lot by marketing agencies was short. In contrast, the eggs placed under refrigeration were owned for an average of several months, requiring much more money per unit to pay not only the original cost of the eggs but also the interest and storage charges upon them. Available evidence indicates that financing frequently is a limiting factor in the accumulation of eggs by many dealers.

Risk also increased greatly under accumulation, both because of the longer period of ownership and the method of price determination. Risks of deterioration and loss could not be disregarded but the main risks were those of price. Obviously, the longer the period of ownership, the greater the risk of loss.

At the outset of the refrigeration of eggs the main risk was that of deterioration of quality during the refrigeration. Price risks were small because eggs could be obtained cheaply in the spring. Since only a few eggs were being refrigerated there was little danger of a loss in price if the quality of the refrigerated eggs was not too poor. This condition changed rapidly, however, as increasing quantities were withdrawn during the spring and competition among dealers for eggs for refrigeration resulted in higher prices for eggs in the spring. Not infrequently, it appears, competition for eggs forced prices in the spring to levels which resulted in losses on egg storage for the season. While risks of deterioration were being cut down by improvements in storage techniques those of price were increasing.

It is true that fluctuations in prices might result in increased profits from accumulations as well as in losses but the possibility of losses ordinarily loomed larger in the minds of prudent dealers because if a heavy loss should force a dealer out of business he would not share in the subsequent profits. Through experience the principle came to be recognized that a prudent dealer should limit his storage commitments to a moderate proportion of his working capital. Then, should losses be suffered, operations could be continued and profits in a following year might overbalance the former losses.

The element of risk likewise affected the cost of financing. A strongly financed company which is able to absorb any probable losses could borrow money for its accumulations of eggs at a relatively low rate but a company which is weak financially might have to pay a higher rate as risk premium. Lending agencies also might refuse to finance more than a specified quantity of inventory for a venturesome dealer.

Price determination under accumulation of eggs differed sharply from the conditions prior to accumulation. Before accumulation the price level was kept closely adjusted to what consumers would pay for the quantities currently offered. Some allowance doubtless was made for the changes expected in the immediate future. Under accumulation, however, the price level for eggs during the period of heavy production was governed primarily by the opinions of dealers concerning the prices which could be obtained for refrigerated (and frozen) eggs during the remainder of the season. Such opinions largely determined the prices for the eggs withdrawn from immediate consumption and, for practical purposes, the price of eggs during flush production. Subsequently, when eggs were being withdrawn from inventories and were competing with fresh eggs, the quantitity of refrigerated eggs on hand and the prices at which they were offered influenced the price of fresh eggs.

This shift in the basis of price determination was highly important. The dealers who accumulated eggs took an active part in the determination of egg prices, particularly during the period of flush production when eggs were accumulated. Furthermore, they were forced by conditions to do so on the basis of incomplete and imperfect information. Most of the Middle West eggs placed under refrigeration were produced in March, April, and May. A dealer accumulating such eggs had to estimate before or during that period how many refrigerated eggs he could sell and what prices he could obtain for them during the remainder of the season in deciding how many eggs to store and what he could pay for the eggs. He might adjust his estimates during his period of accumulation but by the end of May his commitments were largely made. Conditions might change before his eggs are desired by consumers but his accumulation had to be made in advance. In some other areas, such as in the South or in California where the flush season is earlier, the problem of accumulation might be even more difficult.

Lengthening of the egg marketing season should not be overlooked as a result of the accumulation of eggs. It rendered egg marketing more nearly a year round occupation, encouraging wholesale dealers and also retailers and assemblers to devote increased attention to improving its efficiency. Through making refrigerated eggs available to consumers at times when fresh eggs were scarce, accumulation doubtless contributed to an increased consumption of eggs.

Accumulations Of Eggs Became Concentrated

Early in the accumulation of eggs by dealers many of the eggs were owned by numerous interior egg shippers who had erected icehouses. Doubtless there was a wide range in the quality of the refrigerated eggs offered by the various shippers. As the technique of refrigeration improved it appears that the advantage of a large warehouse increased. For example, the use of fans and blowers to promote uniformity of temperature and humidity may not have been practicable in the smaller icehouses. The advantage of the larger warehouses was further apparent with the development of mechanical refrigeration for eggs.

Business reasons also favored concentration. The small shipper with 1 or 2 cars of refrigerated eggs was largely dependent upon brokers in effecting sales to distant buyers whose requirements might vary from year to year. Even if such a shipper were able to offer consistently high quality eggs each year it would be difficult for him to keep his eggs in the memories of a sufficiently large number of buyers. It was easier for buyers at consuming points to deal with companies controlling large quantities of refrigerated eggs.

Another factor favoring the storage of eggs at consuming centers was the greater perishability of refrigerated eggs than of other eggs. This was particularly noticeable if refrigerated eggs were withdrawn from storage in comparatively warm weather, such as might prevail at times in many consuming centers up to the middle of December. Jobbers and other purchasers preferred to buy eggs stored locally in order that small quantities could be withdrawn as needed rather than to purchase a carlot which had been removed from storage and shipped some distance. (57)

As early as 1894 a market report from Chicago in November noted that eggs stored at various country points were quoted at discounts of 2 cents per dozen under those stored at Chicago and it was expected that the discount would widen as the season advanced. (22) A few years later market reports continued to complain of the lack of uniformity in refrigerated eggs stored at country points.

In 1895 it was noted that for several years the Western Cold Storage Company of Chicago had been sending circulars to the smaller egg dealers in the Midwest, setting forth the advantages of storing eggs in its warehouse against the fall demand. (40) Another comment in the same year suggested that the Western had been catering to dealers storing small quantities of eggs. The comment was that the Western was favoring Chicago dealers that season since it was charging 5 cents a case more for small quantities than for a carlot or more and was refusing to advance more than three-fourths of the value of the eggs stored in its warehouse. (40)

A considerable factor in the trend toward the concentration of egg inventories was the entrance of Chicago meat packers into egg storage about the turn of the century. Soon their holdings were important. Shortly before World War I it appears that the eggs in storage at Chicago were owned principally by the Chicago meat packers, Chicago wholesale egg dealers, and a number of interior egg packers, while minor quantities were owned by local jobbers, brokers, speculators, and retailers and some wholesale egg dealers located in other cities.

Still another factor favoring the concentration of the ownership of refrigerated eggs was the advantage of the terminal dealers in judging how many eggs to place under refrigeration and what prices to pay for them each season. In the early stages of egg refrigeration this had been of little consequence but when large quantities of eggs were withdrawn from consumption each spring, causing a sharp increase in the spring price of eggs, judgment as to how many eggs to store and the prices which refrigerated eggs would command became highly important.

The terminal dealers were in a better position than the interior dealers to develop this judgment because they were in touch with both producing and consuming areas and were at centers of information. Although their information was far from perfect, it was easier for them to estimate the quantities of eggs going under refrigeration than for the relatively isolated interior dealers. Being more closely in touch with consuming areas, terminal dealers had better opportunities to appraise the probable demand for refrigerated eggs in a given season. Very likely, also, they could obtain from terminal bankers better indications as to business conditions when the refrigerated eggs would be marketed than the interior dealers could obtain, on the whole, from their local bankers.

In 1939, the first date for which data are available, the ownership of the eggs stored in Chicago was highly concentrated. This statement is based upon the quantities hedged at the end of August which represented about 87 percent of the eggs in storage at Chicago at that time. (50) The hedges were held by only 42 concerns and individuals. Only two country egg shippers were included and their combined holdings amounted to less than 1 percent of the total. It may be concluded that ownership of the eggs at Chicago tended strongly to be concentrated in a relatively small number of terminal egg dealers.

Probably this tendency existed also at other points of accumulation, but perhaps not to the degree disclosed at Chicago. There is reason to believe that the concerns which hedged eggs at Chicago would not have been willing to assume the risks of ownership on that quantity of eggs if they had not been able to hedge.

Outside Speculators Appeared Early

Indications are that speculation in eggs by persons outside the egg business began soon after the technique of shell egg storage had been developed. That this activity was well developed in Chicago by 1895 is indicated by the following item published in that year.

> "At present the indications are that there will be active speculation in eggs this season . . . there are men of moderate means outside the produce business who make a practice of investing in a car or so every year.
>
> "Nearly all these outside investors have friends among the produce houses who act as their agents. Not a great deal of money is required to carry a car of eggs. At 12 cents, it will take 3 cents a dozen, or one-fourth the original cost to be put up by the speculator. The other 9 cents will be advanced by the cold storage companies for the purpose of securing the carrying charges. The latter very often lose money by making a three-quarter advance and the amount of money loaned on eggs varies in different markets." (39)

Such speculation increased materially and attained substantial proportions within the following two decades. Evidently a number of business and professional men were attracted by the sizeable profits made in eggs in some years. As the market developed and the number of outside speculators increased, it appears that most of them came to rely upon egg brokers for the purchase and sale of their eggs although a few may have depended upon friends or relatives in the egg business. Some of the outside speculators probably leaned heavily upon the egg brokers for their judgment as to the purchase of the eggs, the selection of a warehouse and aid in the financing of the transaction, and as to the subsequent sale of the eggs.

On the part of the brokers this service to speculators was carried on in addition to their activities as intermediaries between dealers in eggs. Evidently the business was profitable to brokers with established reputations for they seemed eager to obtain and retain it. The fees charged for their services probably were in keeping with the usual charges for handling eggs, including inspection by the brokers, at terminal markets. Some informants suggest a cent per dozen for each purchase or sale about 1914 but a somewhat lower scale in earlier years.

In theory the initiative in such transactions was taken by the speculator in requesting the expert services of the broker. There is room for the suspicion, however, that some of the brokers were ingenious in suggesting the chance of profits to potential patrons, particularly to those who might deal in a number of cars.

Developments In Butter Were Similar

Although the full story of the development of the butter market would exceed the limits of this paper a few comments may be helpful. Almost within the memories of veteran butter merchants the butter which could not be sold immediately to consumers was carried forward, first by farmers in their spring houses and, a little later, by country stores. The surplus butter was salted heavily and held until it could be sold. A few years later the seasonal surplus was commonly held by commission houses for the account of the shippers. Settlement for it was not made until the butter was sold.

An interesting variation was the practice of some families of buying a tub or more of June dairy butter and putting it in their cellars for use during the following winter. (58) Presumably better quality could be obtained in this way than by taking what might be offered by the grocer next winter.

As competition for butter among commission merchants became keener, various inducements were offered to obtain the shipments of some of the country stores which had reputations for unusually good butter. Although details are lacking, it appears that some commission merchants began to make cash advances to obtain such shipments. Later came the outright purchase of butter for storage. With the increased use of refrigeration the butter moved from the cellars of commission merchants to cold storage warehouses. Presently nearly all the seasonal surplus of butter came to be owned by butter merchants, principally at the wholesale level.

Time Contracts Arose To Meet New Needs

The growth of the egg market in size and complexity and, especially, the accumulation of eggs by dealers set the stage for time contracts in egg marketing. At the outset they were like any other contracts which pass unnoticed in the daily course of ordinary business. It was not until they were employed extensively by dealers in their attempts to cope with the changing problems of egg marketing that these contracts attracted attention. The first definite reference to them at Chicago in trade journals was early in 1897 although there is evidence that by then they had been in use for some time. A Chicago dispatch in 1895 stated that there had been a great deal of such trading 10 or 12 years before, probably on the Chicago Produce Exchange after it was revived in 1882, but that it had died out. (38) At that time there seems to have been only a little storing of eggs.

Two types of time contracts took form in egg marketing. The first type called for the delivery of refrigerated eggs in the fall or early winter. It provided a way by which an egg dealer who had accumulated a large inventory of refrigerated eggs could reduce his risks. One such instance was that of a prominent shipper in one of the last settled areas of Iowa who entered into such contracts extensively as early as 1887, soon after he began the refrigeration of eggs on a large scale. Use of such contracts aided him in expanding his storage operations, helping his business to keep pace with the increase in production in his territory. In a few years he had such contracts with dealers in New York, New England, in the Northwest, and on the Pacific Coast. It is possible that this type of time contract may have been employed even earlier by dealers in older sections.

The other type of time contract was used in obtaining eggs for placing under refrigeration. Such eggs should be of better quality than the ordinary market arrivals. Wholesale egg dealers, principally at eastern markets, desired to obtain eggs for storage from shippers who had achieved reputations for packs of superior quality and entered into contracts calling for a specified number of cars of eggs of a given pack, perhaps with some additional specifications as to quality. These contracts commonly were made in the late winter or early spring, many of them at the meetings of the various State associations of egg shippers. They were for delivery in the spring months specified, mainly in April. Some of the smaller eastern dealers who wanted only one or two cars commissioned brokers to find them a good pack.

Frequently the early contracts of this type were informal, being based largely on the confidence engendered by previous dealings and by reputation in the trade. After haggling over prices, quality, packages, etc., the parties would agree upon terms. In many instances each would merely make a memorandum of the transaction to refresh his memory.

Time contracts of this type became numerous late in the 1890s'. Demand for refrigerated eggs was increasing and the brokers representing the smaller dealers had to seek out new egg shippers who were developing good quality packs since the established shippers usually preferred to deal in larger units with the larger eastern egg dealers.

By 1900 such contracts were common in Chicago. The preceding year it was reported that, "The tendency to buy and sell futures in eggs is increasing alarmingly. A few years ago it was done to some extent by a few speculators, but this year we find many old established firms doing it." (42)

On March 6, 1900 a car of storage-packed eggs sold at 11 cents per dozen on the open board after another car had been offered at 11½ cents with no takers. (43)

During the first part of the present century the volume of time contracts at Chicago increased materially. It was particularly easy for brokers to enter into them since frequently a broker would be commissioned to enter into such contracts for certain of his clients. If he chanced to be offered a few additional cars on favorable terms there was always the possibility that other clients might take them off his hands. In such circumstances it was easy to pass from the hope of additional brokerage fees to speculative ventures. Trading in time contracts, principally in those calling for spring delivery, became extensive also in other egg-marketing centers; perhaps mainly in New York but also in a number of cities in the Middle West.

It should be noted, however, that although the volume of these contracts was substantial, it was small in proportion to the cash transactions in eggs. Most of the eggs were handled outside the time contracts and the persons entering into such contracts constituted only a minority, although an influential one, among egg dealers.

Time Contracts Showed Evolution

By approximately 1917 a considerable degree of development was evident in the Chicago time contracts. Standard forms which had been worked out through varied experiences largely replaced the crude memoranda of early days. As to quality, grades developed by the Chicago Butter and Egg Board were used generally instead of the packs of the various shippers. Use of these grades favored another development, the transfer of contracts from one trader to another. Such transfers began as early as 1900 but later they became common and sometimes "rings" would be formed with some contracts changing hands a dozen times or more during periods of relatively large price changes.

In addition, the attitude toward the contracts became less personal. At the outset they had been personal affairs and it had been expected that each contract would be fulfilled by delivery. When "rings" were formed it sometimes happened that the maker of a contract to sell, for example, might purchase it, settling the contract by the payment of a difference in price. The proportion of unfulfilled contracts at times of sharp price changes increased, perhaps in part because when contracts were general it was more difficult to restrict them to persons of responsibility.

Another change had to do with the fulfillment of the time contracts. They continued to call for delivery and acceptance of the eggs but, if both parties to a contract were willing, one or the other might redeem his commitment by payment of an agreed sum, perhaps the difference in the market price. Presently a financial settlement came to be made in a number of instances instead of delivery and acceptance. Indications are that this practice was most common at the larger markets, perhaps because the traders there had more opportunities of this type than did those in smaller places.

Exchanges Attempted To Exercise Some Control

Most time contracts in eggs among Chicago and New York dealers probably were made on the floors of the respective exchanges where dealers congregated although some were made elsewhere. At Chicago, it appears that many were made at one or two taverns frequented by egg dealers. Presently the contracts made on the floors of the exchanges were given official attention. The exchanges did not take official notice of the contracts made between their members and nonmember egg packers.

By 1911 the rules of the Chicago Butter and Egg Board provided that margins of as much as $1.00 a case on time contracts in eggs might be demanded by either party to such contracts. Further efforts are reported by Nourse, writing about 1917. He stated that members of the Chicago Butter and Egg Board had been dealing in futures at the daily "call" for delivery the following day, the next week, or some more distant date. This practice was the subject of controversy and on March 19, 1915 the Board voted, as an experiment, to discontinue such trading for sixty days. After five weeks, however, the trading was resumed, but with the qualification that the contracts were to be limited to ten days. Then in July, 1916 the Board voted almost unanimously to allow members to buy and sell for delivery at any time in the future, but that all contracts for more than ten days in the future must be in writing, signed by both parties, and that a margin of approximately a cent per dozen (a cent per pound for butter) must be deposited with the treasurer of the Board. Contracts were to be made by future months and were to be either "seller's option" or "buyer's option". (60)

At New York, steps toward control of the trading in time contracts had been taken earlier than at Chicago. By approximately 1900, the New York Mercantile Exchange had provided that sales of butter or eggs made on the exchange for future delivery should be evidenced by a standard contract signed by both parties and that margins equal to 10 percent of the contract price should be deposited by both parties with the Superintendant of the Exchange. (71) Provision was made also for additional margins, if necessary. The contract showed the commodity, quantity, grade, price, and terms of delivery, together with the names and addresses of both parties. Contracts could be transferred from one trader to another; notice to the Exchange of such transfers was provided for but was not enforced.

Thus some efforts to control the trading in time contracts were evident at the two principal centers of egg and butter marketing in the United States. Evidently there were wide differences of opinion concerning the value of that trading. It is significant that at Chicago an attempt was made to abolish trading in time contracts.[5]

Requirement of margin deposits on the contracts, both at Chicago and New York, is particularly interesting since the first rule dealing with the time contracts in grain at Chicago provided that margins of up to 10 percent might be demanded by either party to such a contract. This rule was adopted by the Board of Trade in May, 1865. The prominence of rules providing

[5] See p. 42 for a statement of an attempt in 1922 to abolish or greatly restrict organized trading in butter and egg futures at Chicago.

No corresponding attempt to abolish trading in time contracts in butter and eggs at New York was found but it was not practicable to make as intensive a study of developments in butter and egg marketing at New York as at Chicago.

for margin deposits suggests that difficulties with the fulfillment of time contracts were not uncommon among the members of the various exchanges. Subsequent developments suggest that the adoption of such rules was none too effective in assuring the fulfillment of the contracts.

Time Contracts Facilitated Egg Marketing

In retrospect, it is evident that in spite of their imperfections the time contracts were helpful to the expanding egg trade. Undoubtedly the trading in such contracts was carried to excess by a number of egg brokers and other traders but on the whole the contracts aided interior egg packers, wholesalers, and jobbers in solving the new problems posed by the rapid changes in egg marketing, particularly the problems which arose from the increasing accumulation of eggs.

Time contracts calling for delivery in the fall helped the interior egg shipper in expanding his storage operations to keep pace with increasing production in his territory. By entering into them, he was able to increase his holdings of eggs under refrigeration more rapidly than would have been prudent otherwise. His accumulation of eggs gave rise to inter-related problems of storage, financing, and risk assumption. The time contracts reduced his price risks and aided in obtaining financing on more favorable terms. Presumably, also, the prices agreed upon were attractive to the purchasers and both shippers and purchasers were benefitted by assured outlets and sources of supply.

Perhaps the contracts for fall delivery were relatively most important in the early days of accumulation of eggs when large quantities in the aggregate were stored by egg shippers in their own icehouses at interior points. As the accumulation of eggs shifted toward terminals (see pp. 25-28) there may have been less advantage in the fall contracts.

Likewise, the time contracts calling for the delivery

of storage packed eggs in the spring served the needs of the egg shippers and of the dealers who purchased the eggs. From the shipper's standpoint, the ability to arrange in advance for part of his pack permitted him to make more definite plans for his early spring season. If he had achieved a reputation for an unusually good pack, the reputation was likely to be reflected in the contract price. From the standpoint of the purchaser, the contracts aided in arranging for eggs packed for refrigeration, of specified quality, from a preferred locality, and produced during an agreed period.

Furthermore, the prices stated in the spring contracts were helpful to the trade generally in arriving at the price level of eggs during the flush season. The prices agreed upon in the contracts between well-known egg shippers and leading wholesale dealers affected the market level strongly at the opening of the season of flush production since many others tended to accept the judgment of the leaders. Of course, developments during the season might prove that the earlier prices were too high or too low. (Frequently the competition among dealers for eggs for storage forced prices above the conservative level established at the opening of the season.) A level had to be established, however, and the time contracts facilitated arriving at it. As stated, (see pp. 24-25) the estimates of dealers concerning the prices which could be obtained for refrigerated eggs the following fall and winter exerted an increased influence upon egg prices in the fall and early summer as larger quantities of eggs were withdrawn from immediate consumption during the flush period and placed under refrigeration.

At terminal markets the trading in time contracts permitted traders to accept their profits or limit their losses more readily than would have been possible otherwise, thus aiding them to limit their risks. It also permitted them to conduct a larger business with a given capital than would have been equally prudent in the absence of that trading.

The trading also facilitated the marketing of eggs in some minor ways. As one example, sometimes it was more convenient to contract to sell eggs for delivery in the following fall or winter than to make an outright sale of eggs held in storage. If the property changed hands it might have been necessary to arrange for a new loan and to transfer the insurance.

Organized Trading Was The Next Step

The measures adopted by the Chicago Butter and Egg Board to control the unorganized trading in time contracts among its members were of little avail in 1917 when prices shot upward, especially after the entrance of the United States into World War I. Many contracts were not fulfilled.

Before the United States had declared war, the volume of time contracts had increased materially. Numerous dealers and brokers were willing to contract to buy eggs at rising prices. When the United States entered the war, prices advanced sharply and trading in contracts showed further expansion. Large profits and losses were common. As an extreme example, a well-known Chicago concern bought on April 25, a contract for 50 cars of Storage Packed Firsts at 33½ cents and sold it the following day at 36 cents per dozen, making a net profit of nearly $15,000.00.

Most of the contracts were fulfilled, although losses were heavy in some instances, but in a number of contracts delivery was not made. In other contracts the eggs delivered were inferior in quality. Failure to deliver was especially noticeable in a number of the rings in which time contracts changed hands, frequently several times. If one party in the chain failed to make delivery or to pay the difference in price, the whole ring might collapse. Each of the successive parties might claim that he could not make delivery because he had not received delivery or the price agreed to be paid him. Many disputes arose and a number of lawsuits were begun, principally as means of attempting to force settlements.

In 1917 also the contracts for fall and winter delivery were affected by the Food Control Act which became effective on August 10. In response to an inquiry from Chicago as to those contracts, the Food Administration stated on December 13 that time contracts were contrary to its rules and regulations and prohibited buyers from accepting eggs on such contracts in excess of the reasonable requirements of each. The Food Administration expressed no opinion as to the financial rights or responsibilities of the parties to the contracts.

In 1918 there was no trading in time contracts for butter or eggs because of the prohibitions of the Food Control Act. In 1919 trading was resumed but again there was wide spread dissatisfaction because of nonfulfillment of contracts, largely because of sharp price advances.

It was evident that a complete set of trading rules would be needed to assure the fulfillment of time contracts. Since earlier efforts to promote control of time contracts by the Chicago Butter and Egg Board had resulted in only minor changes in the rules of that body it seemed unlikely that such rules could be set up within the board. Apparently those who were interested in time contracts were a minority.

Late in the spring of 1919 a number of members of the Board gathered in one of the Board rooms one afternoon to await the outcome of an attempt to settle a strike of egg candlers. A group resumed the discussion of ways of handling the trading in time contracts and finally agreed to ask Mr. W. S. Moore to form an independent association for organized trading in butter and egg futures.

Committees were appointed to obtain information concerning the organized trading in grain, cotton, and other commodities. Their findings were reported to a central committee which drafted the rules and regulations for a new exchange. Plans were going forward for a separate organization but presently, in order to avoid having two organizations of butter and egg men at Chicago the Chicago Butter and Egg Board agreed to add the rules for organized futures trading to its other rules and to permit the group to operate as a unit within the Board.

The new organization was called the Chicago Mercantile Exchange since it might become desirable to trade in some other commodity futures as well as in butter and egg futures. The Chicago Butter and Egg Board went out of existence on October 5; on October 6 the Chicago Mercantile Exchange began operations, although organized trading in butter and egg futures did not begin until December 1, 1919. Most of the memberships of the Chicago Butter and Egg Board were transferred to the new organization, although there were some slight changes in the ways in which memberships were held. The officers of the Chicago Butter and Egg Board continued as officers of the Chicago Mercantile Exchange until the following January.

Futures Trading Was Only One Department

The Chicago Mercantile Exchange continued the activities of the Chicago Butter and Egg Board. In addition a group, termed the Clearing House, was set up in the Exchange to handle the organized trading in butter and egg futures. Membership in the Clearing House was open to any member of the Exchange who could meet the requirements, including a deposit of $500.00 as a reserve against possible losses, but many of the members of the Exchange were not interested in being members of the Clearing House. Some were content with existing conditions, some were not interested in organized trading in futures, while others felt that there were too many risks involved because the Clearing House undertook to guarantee all futures contracts, once they had been accepted by its manager, and if the losses should exceed the reserve fund the excess would be shared among the members of the Clearing House.

The new rules governing the Clearing House set forth that the Exchange should maintain a Clearing House, that the executive secretary of the Exchange should be the business manager of the Clearing House under the Clearing House Committee, and that the Clearing House Committee should have full power over the operations of the Clearing House, subject to the Board of Directors of the Chicago Mercantile Exchange. To reduce to a minimum the danger of losses to the Clearing House it was provided that margins should be deposited with it by both parties to each contract cleared, and that the margin should be adjusted each day to the market price. Provision was made also that a member of the Clearing House trading for customers must collect margins from each customer. Penalties were provided for defaults on contracts.

All futures transactions made on the Exchange were required to be cleared. Members of the Exchange but not of the Clearing House were required to clear all futures transactions through members of the Clearing House. A new and more definite set of grades for butter and for eggs was established by the Exchange (there were no Federal grades) and a well staffed inspection department was provided.

The establishment of the Clearing House was accepted without noticeable dissent but soon its operations aroused considerable opposition. Naturally there was resentment on the part of brokers who had been representing speculators in the purchase and sale of butter and eggs and who found that the speculators could trade through the Clearing House members for a quarter of a cent per pound or per dozen instead of perhaps 2 cents or more to a broker. Some Exchange members who had been accustomed to making contracts casually may have disliked the requirement that all futures contracts made on the Exchange must be cleared. Some of the wholesale houses, too, may have lost some business to the Clearing House; e.g. an egg jobber might accept delivery of a car of eggs instead of purchasing it from a given wholesaler.

Opposition to the Clearing House increased in 1921 and 1922 as the Clearing House operations increased in volume. Near the close of 1922 a determined effort was made to abolish the Clearing House, or at least to restrict its operations. In the meantime the value of organized trading had been demonstrated and its adherents agreed that, if necessary, they would withdraw from the Chicago Mercantile Exchange and set up a separate organization. Faced with this alternative, the opposition subsided. (9) Organized trading, though relatively undeveloped, had become a firmly established feature of the Chicago Mercantile Exchange.

Organized Trading Underwent Evolution

Organized trading in butter and egg futures gained rapidly, both in volume of trading and in the aggregates of contracts held open. Within two decades it was the predominant activity of the Exchange. In contrast the sales of butter and eggs through the "spot call" and the relative importance of the inspections of butter and eggs have been much reduced. By 1940 only small quantities of butter and eggs were sold on the "spot call", with the exception of Government purchases of butter as a price support. This decrease resulted principally from changes in the marketing of butter and eggs. These changes also affected the inspection of butter and eggs which, by 1940, was principally one of the services subsidiary to futures trading.

The number of open contracts in both butter and eggs increased more rapidly than their respective volumes of transactions. The open contracts in a given future refer to the contracts in effect; i.e. those which have been made but have not been settled by offset or by delivery. In the early days of the Exchange the average daily volume of trading was equal to approximately one-tenth of the average aggregate of open contracts; about 1940 it was about one-sixteenth. In egg futures the comparable reduction was from about one-eighth to one-fourteenth. The decreased ratios may be attributed largely to the development of hedging since many hedging positions are held for several months. There may also have been a decrease in scalping and less switching from one future to another than in the early days.

Another change was the sharp decrease in the importance of non-refrigerated butter and egg futures. At the outset, numerous futures calling for the delivery of fresh butter and fresh eggs were provided. As late as 1923, the first year for which data of trading had been compiled, there were 11 fresh butter and 9 fresh egg futures in addition to 4 futures calling for the delivery of storage packed eggs. Storage packed eggs are eggs packed for refrigeration, usually in new fillers and flats and frequently in new cases. Dirty and checked eggs are excluded and the pack is graded. Even in 1923 the refrigerated futures made up nearly 80 percent of the open contracts in both butter and eggs.

Very likely the "fresh" futures were set up and traded in the hope that in some way they would prove to be valuable. As the traders gained in experience, most of the "fresh" futures were discontinued. By 1940 the refrigerated futures represented more than 98 percent of the open contracts in both butter and eggs. The rate of change between the kinds of futures is shown below by the proportions which each type made up of the aggregate of open contracts every fourth year, 1923-1939.

	1923	1927	1931	1935	1939
	Percent	Percent	Percent	Percent	Percent
Butter futures					
Refrigerated	78.3	93.2	95.7	97.4	99.7
Fresh	21.7	6.8	4.3	2.6	0.3
Egg futures					
Refrigerated	77.7	89.1	95.5	96.9	98.2
Storage-packed	18.0	4.0	4.3	1.8	1.2
Fresh	4.3	6.9	0.2	1.3	0.6

It is evident that there was an increase in the refrigerated futures and a decrease in the others. It may be inferred that in most instances the advantages of the fresh futures did not equal their costs. Limited advantages are discernible in the storage-packed futures which are used in obtaining eggs for refrigeration and in the January and February fresh egg futures which may be useful at times in guarding against "weather markets". A Midwest egg shipper who fears that mild weather may increase egg production sharply and cause prices to drop before the eggs which he is purchasing can reach terminal markets may contract to sell against that contingency.

While part of the shift in types of futures may have resulted from the changes in the marketing of cash butter and eggs, it is believed that most of it was caused by the development of hedging. No evidence of hedging was found at the beginning of organized trading in butter and egg futures. The primary concern of the supporters of organized trading was to assure the fulfillment of contracts. Evidently it was considered that the main function of the futures market would be the exchange of ownership through delivery upon the contracts or the assurance of profits (or losses) through changes in the price level. An editorial in "Dairy Produce" at the beginning of organized trading noted that the leaders hoped that the Clearing House would serve as an improved means of exchange. Likewise, the advertising of the Clearing House early in 1920 pointed with pride to the number of contracts cleared satisfactorily and emphasized that in the April future no disputes had arisen to require arbitration.

Not only was there no evidence of hedging immediately after the beginning of organized trading in butter and egg futures but also there was hardly any interest in it. Dealers, generally, were looking for speculative profits in accumulating butter and eggs. On the whole, such storage had been profitable for many years in spite of heavy losses in some years. One of the leading Chicago concerns is reported to have operated on the theory, based on observation, that out of 7 years the distribution of profits was likely to be:

3 years of profits, some large
2 years of small profits or losses
2 years of losses, sometimes heavy

The concern was careful to maintain adequate reserves against the possible losses and expected that on the whole the profits would overbalance the losses. Most other dealers who accumulated butter and eggs seemed to think that accumulation was profitable although losses would be suffered in some years.

One firm began to hedge its accumulations a few years after organized trading began, primarily in an effort to attain a larger volume of business in proportion to the firm's financial resources than the partners felt would be prudent without hedging. Other dealers, however, did not seem much interested in the practice. Several of them made such comments as, "Last year you handled 200 cars. We made as much money as you did and we handled only 50 cars." Such attitudes, of course, overlooked the fact that the profits on the smaller quantities included speculative profits which might turn into losses in some years.

Interest in hedging increased greatly in 1930 and 1931 after heavy losses had been suffered by dealers in butter and eggs on the quantities accumulated in 1929 and 1930, largely as a result of the depression which began late in 1929. It was reported that some of the dealers had difficulty in financing their accumulations. In such circumstances the advantage of transferring price risks on accumulations became more evident, both to the dealers and to their bankers.

Incomplete evidence as to the increase in hedging is afforded by the comparison of open contracts in eggs and butter, respectively, with the stocks under refrigeration at Chicago at the close of the principal storing season of each over a period of 19 years, ended in 1940. The stocks in storage at Chicago rather than for the United States are cited because comparatively little of the eggs or butter stored outside Chicago was hedged. The data are:

Year	Eggs		Butter	
	Open Contracts	Stocks in storage at Chicago	Open contracts storage standards (and extras)	Stocks in storage at Chicago
	May 31		July 31	
	Carlots	Carlots	Carlots	Carlots
1922	526	3,250	321	1,262
1923	818	3,220	371	913
1924	591	2,882	579	1,181
1925	1,614	2,780	1,230	1,332
1926	1,187	3,035	1,190	1,526
1927	2,690	3,780	1,278	1,447
1928	2,374	3,365	892	1,114
1929	1,695	3,222	646	1,381
1930	1,286	3,730	1,506	1,551
1931	1,123	3,362	1,273	1,439
1932	1,194	2,195	836	1,108
1933	1,876	4,490	1,747	1,926
1934	1,991	4,388	1,226	1,382
1935	1,939	3,422	1,512	2,212
1936	1,437	2,535	1,555	1,246
1937	2,202	3,318	1,352	1,570
1938	2,918	3,748	1,701	2,287[1]
1939	3,410	3,600	1,401	2,681[1]
1940	2,300	3,868	1,308	1,436

[1] Substantial quantities of butter in storage at Chicago on these dates were held by Governmental and quasi-Governmental agencies.

It is evident that in the first three years the open contracts were small relative to the quantities in storage at the end of the principal storing season. Obviously the hedging of the stocks in store could not exceed the short side of the open contracts; it could be zero. Some of the short positions in the 3 years doubtless represented advance sales made to establish a price for later delivery.

A sharp increase in the open contracts relative to the stocks in storage is apparent in 1925. Thereafter the trend was irregular but in general it was in the direction of greater open contracts in proportion to the stocks in storage. Presumably nearly all the short positions represented sales by butter and egg dealers against actual or anticipated holdings since analysis of holdings toward the close of the period shown disclosed only a very small proportion of speculative short sales.

By 1939 the characteristic pattern of the open contracts had become one of hedging positions on the short side and speculative positions on the long side. On August 31, 1939 there were 1,165 traders on the long side of Chicago egg futures to 54 on the short side, including 12 who held small speculative short positions. (50) In butter futures on the same date there were 360 on the long side and 33 on the short side, including 3 traders with speculative short positions. (51) More than 97 percent of the short positions in egg futures and 99 percent in butter futures were hedges. In both butter and eggs nearly all the hedges were held by Chicago concerns, principally in large units while the traders holding long positions were widely scattered geographically and most of their positions were small. In both butter and egg futures more than 80 percent of the long positions was held by traders drawn from the butter and egg business and related industries.

In contrast to the early trading in time contracts in which contracts were settled by delivery, hedging contemplates that typically the price risks will be transferred to others by means of the futures contracts, but that the commodity involved will be retained by the hedger for merchandising or processing, and that the futures contracts will subsequently be settled by offsetting futures transactions. Dealers who purchase for forward delivery in order to obtain possession of a commodity would not ordinarily be willing to have their contracts settled by offset; hence the presence of a large body of speculators who do not desire to accept delivery is required if hedging is practiced extensively.

Speculators from outside the butter and egg business were found in butter and egg marketing long before the beginning of organized trading in butter and egg futures. Their presence at Chicago was noted as early as 1895 (see 40) and they doubtless increased in number in the following 15 years. It is reasonable to conclude also that speculators in butter and eggs increased during the first decade of organized futures trading. It was cheaper and more convenient to speculate in butter and eggs under organized trading than formerly when a speculator had to depend upon the personal guidance and assistance of a broker.

The number of speculators from outside the butter and egg business probably was increased materially after about 1931 when the Exchange endeavored to attract such speculators in order to take the other side of the increasing hedges. A number of futures commission merchants dealing in other commodity futures and in securities were encouraged to become members of the Chicago Mercantile Exchange and to solicit trades in butter and egg futures. Efforts were made also to educate their local solicitors in butter and eggs. In the aggregate these commission merchants who came into the Exchange had branches in a large number of cities and towns throughout the United States and were in a position to solicit a large group of potential speculators. Probably their activities added materially to the number of speculators who held long positions in butter and egg futures.

As of August 31, 1939 about 20 percent of the long positions in butter futures and 30 percent of those in egg futures were held by persons outside the butter and egg business and related industries. Another 20 percent in butter futures and 10 percent in egg futures were held by persons in the related industries, such as cold storage, meat packing, cheese handling, ice cream manufacture, and the produce business. Only about 60 percent of the long positions in either butter or egg futures was held by persons in the butter and egg business. (50) (51)

Another factor in the evolution of organized trading in butter and eggs was the increased degree of control exercised over manipulation. Shortly after organized trading began, some members discovered that the penalties for defaults on futures contracts could be used for manipulation. Penalties for defaulting on contracts had been set on the severe side as one means of assuring fulfillment of futures contracts and some traders saw how these penalties could be used to "squeeze the shorts" and push prices to artificially high levels at times in expiring futures by insisting upon delivery of unexpectedly large quantities. Several "squeezes" were engineered, mainly in eggs, which met with disapproval of forward-looking members and attracted unfavorable public and governmental comment.

It is true that a number of the members of the Exchange took the stand that if a trader were able to operate a "squeeze" or a "corner", it was a private matter between him and the shorts who were being squeezed and that the Exchange should not interfere. They pointed out that "squeezes" were not then prohibited on some of the older exchanges. Perhaps some of these members had a personal interest in the practice, either in the hope of obtaining profits through a successful "squeeze" or in the expectation of brokerage from the transactions involved in the squeeze. Such short-sighted views, however, were not shared by the majority of the membership.

It was generally recognized that manipulation reduced the value of trading in organized futures in the marketing of a given commodity, obscuring its true value and interfering with the orderly fulfillment of contracts. Various measures, growing largely out of experience, were adopted in an effort to control squeezes. Contracts were widened to include an increased number of grades at appropriate price differentials and provision was made for delivery in designated warehouses at points outside Chicago. New rules governing the settlement of defaulted futures contracts provided for a sliding scale of penalties, ranging from 1/8 cent to 3 cents per pound or per dozen, over the fair market value of the contracts defaulted. The fair market value is determined by one committee, the appropriate penalty by another committee which is instructed to consider the circumstances affecting the default. These provisions are much like those of the Liverpool Corn Trade Association which was remarkably successful in avoiding "squeezes" and "corners". (72)

Organized Trading Facilitated Butter And Egg Marketing

Examination of marketing practices leads to the conclusion that organized trading in butter and egg futures added materially to the efficiency of the marketing of both commodities. The services rendered by this trading were principally in connection with the seasonal accumulations of butter and eggs but improvements in the marketing of refrigerated butter and eggs also aided in the merchandising of fresh butter and eggs, particularly during the respective periods of accumulation. Organized trading likewise made a small contribution to the marketing of fresh eggs (see pp. 44; 59). It is true that the services of organized trading were rendered mainly for the butter and eggs stored at Chicago but because Chicago was the central reservoir for refrigerated butter and eggs the effects of those services extended far beyond Chicago.

Perhaps the most convenient way of appraising the value of organized trading in butter and egg futures is to analyze each of the marketing services which it rendered, even though discussion of the individual services tends to obscure the inter-relationships between some of them. Organized trading facilitated the marketing of butter and eggs in the following ways:

1. It aided in the transfer of price risks
2. It aided in financing accumulations, increasing competition
3. It aided in price determination
4. It promoted an improved price structure
5. It assisted in transfer of ownership
6. It provided quotations suitable for wide dissemination
7. It furnished a continuous market

Organized trading aided in the transfer of price risks. At first it aided primarily by assuring the fulfillment of contracts and facilitating the making (and offsetting) of contracts; subsequently it made hedging possible, thus extending the transfer of risks.

Some price risks had been transferred through time contracts long before the beginning of organized trading in butter and egg futures but the value of such transfers had been cut down by the uncertainty of fulfillment at times of sharp price changes when protection against price risks was most needed. When fulfillment was assured under organized trading the transfer of price risks probably was increased, especially since organized trading added to the convenience and economy of such contracts. Indications are, however, that the volume of such transfers was not more than moderate.

When hedging became general an increased proportion of the price risks of accumulations of butter and eggs was transferred from dealers to others. One of the factors in the increase may well have been a gain in the number of traders who were willing to take the other side of the hedges. Presumably more people are willing to assume the price risks in the hope of profit than are in a position to take over the ownership and resale of a car of butter or eggs, particularly if the resale must be handled by an agent.

Here the term "transfer" is used in a qualified sense. It does not imply that the risks which are passed on by a given dealer represent the same aggregate to those who assume them. On the contrary the value of such risks to those others may be quite different, particularly since risks frequently are highly concentrated in dealers' hands.

Large proportions of the price risks incurred in the accumulation of butter and eggs at Chicago were transferred to others in 1939 but only a small fraction of the risks incurred by the accumulations in the United States were transferred. The influence of hedging was greater than the proportions shown on p. 46 would indicate because a number of dealers assumed some price risks, hedging only the quantities in excess of the risks which they were willing or able to assume.

Before organized trading began, many concerns were willing to accumulate given quantities which they felt able to carry without undue risks. Additional quantities would be purchased only at price concessions, even though other conditions should be unchanged. Thus a small surplus toward the end of a storing season might have a disproportionate effect upon prices if it were market-wide; if only a few concerns were involved those offering the excess quantities might have to find other takers. Such a condition is less likely to arise under organized trading.

Hedging permitted greater flexibility in butter and egg marketing. In contrast to the time contracts in which delivery on the contracts was customary, hedging permitted the dealers to transfer their price risks only, retaining possession of the commodity for merchandising according to the best opportunities available at the time of merchandising. It should be noted, however, that while hedging afforded the dealer using it definite advantages over the time contracts, it might not always afford as complete protection in the event that the futures prices failed to move substantially in unison with the cash prices of the commodity hedged. Should cash prices decline and futures price advance, the protection afforded by hedging would be reduced.

Organized trading aided in financing the accumulations of butter and eggs, thus permitting more active competition on the part of a number of expanding butter and egg dealers. Through reducing the price risks of accumulations it tended to decrease the capital required in accumulating a given quantity of butter or eggs. More money can be borrowed upon hedged than unhedged holdings and, more important, the quantity of a commodity which can be carried forward prudently increases under hedging. Perhaps 10 to 20 percent more will be lent, on an average, upon a commodity if it is hedged than if it is not. Prudent dealers, however, may not always wish to assume all the risks which their banks may permit.

The difference between the financing of a commodity which commonly is hedged and one which then could not be hedged is brought out by an estimate of the financing of cotton and of wool. It was held that a wool marketing concern would not hold wool to the extent of more than twice its capital while a cotton marketing concern which hedged could hold cotton to the extent of five times its capital. (55) Admittedly, this comparison was made in an effort to present cotton futures in a favorable light but merchants generally agree that with a given capital they are willing to accumulate a larger quantity of a commodity hedged than if it could not be hedged.

Reduction of risks also permitted the funds needed in the financing of inventories of butter and eggs to be borrowed on more favorable terms.* It is generally recognized that the greater the risks the higher the rate of interest. In addition to lowered interest rates, reduced risks may aid in financing through such matters as lessening arrangements for giving security.

Organized trading also contributed to the financing of butter and egg accumulations by cold storage warehouses. In some instances some of such warehouses would provide all or nearly all the funds to pay for the butter or eggs placed in them by certain dealers, and the warehouse would hedge the commodities. The butter or eggs were held for the account of the respective dealer who would endeavor to merchandise the commodities during the following fall or winter. If he could do so, he could pay for the commodity, plus accrued storage and any other costs; if he could not merchandise the commodity the warehouse would deliver it upon the hedging contracts. This practice was used primarily by some cold storage warehouses to bring in more butter and eggs on which to earn storage charges; on the other hand it was helpful to certain butter and egg dealers who otherwise might not have been able to accumulate butter or eggs or could do so only to a limited extent.

This practice of financing storage holdings did not originate with organized trading in butter and egg futures. Before 1895 it was noted that cold storage warehouses were advancing as much as three-quarters of the original cost of a car of eggs for refrigeration. (39) One of the services rendered 20 years later by brokers

*Author's opinion.

to speculators in butter and eggs was assistance in financing, frequently through cold storage warehouses, and doubtless the trade of dealers in butter and eggs was sought by warehouses with financing as one of the attractions. Under organized trading, however, the warehouses were able to make their arrangements with greater precision.

Reduction in the capital required to carry forward the accumulations of butter and eggs cut down the advantage formerly enjoyed by the strongly financed concerns in accumulating inventories of those commodities and permitted more aggressive competition on the part of expanding concerns which possessed only moderate capital. Thus organized trading increased the part which merchandising ability and business judgment played in butter and egg marketing.

It is impracticable to attempt to determine the relative importance of financing and the transfer of risks upon the marketing of butter and eggs but there is reason to believe that together they contributed to a considerable reduction in the margins obtained for the storage of those commodities. It is recognized that decreased seasonality of production and other technological developments also contributed to the reduced margins and that the lower prices which prevailed in the latter part of the period studied were a factor but it appears that organized trading in butter and egg futures were definitely a factor in the decreased margins from 1920 through 1939.

The margin for butter was reduced from about 4 cents to a little more than 1 cent per pound and that for eggs from nearly 4 cents to 1.4 cents per dozen. The margin for butter each year was computed by taking the average difference in price in July between the price of Fresh Standards and the average July quotation for the November or December future (whichever was quoted in July that year); in eggs the price difference between the October (or November) future and Storage Packed Firsts during May each year was taken. In order to smooth out the variations from one year to another, a five-year moving average of the margins was computed, centering on the years shown. The data for 1920-1939 are:

Average Storage Margins Of Butter And Eggs[1]

Year	Butter	Eggs
Five year moving average centered on	Cents per pound	Cents per dozen
1922	4.0	3.7
1923	3.7	3.3
1924	3.2	3.3
1925	2.9	3.4
1926	2.8	3.4
1927	2.8	3.4
1928	2.9	3.6
1929	2.7	3.6
1930	2.4	3.3
1931	2.3	3.3
1932	2.1	2.8
1933	1.5	2.3
1934	1.3	1.8
1935	1.3	1.8
1936	1.1	1.5
1937	1.1	1.4
1938	1.1	1.4

Since the change was gradual the spreads shown for 1922 may be taken as typical for those of the first few years. A pronounced reduction in the margins between 1929 and 1933, when prices declined sharply, is evident but the downward trend is apparent at other times as well.

[1] In eggs the October future was not traded until 1932 and in butter the November future was not traded until 1930. In two of the early years the December egg future was used because the November egg futures were not traded. This difference in the months may have affected storage costs slightly but the effects of the difference are believed to have been small, particularly in eggs since many eggs were stored on a seasonal rate.

Organized trading aided in the determination of butter and egg prices, primarily during the respective periods of accumulation but also during the periods of withdrawal from storage. Futures quotations are arrived at publicly in open trading under definite procedures which tend to bring all price-making factors into focus. Prices warranted by existing conditions are difficult to arrive at during periods of accumulation because they have to be based on incomplete information as to conditions during the remainder of the respective marketing years. This condition developed long before the beginning of organized trading. (see pp. 23-25). All that the trading could contribute was a greater degree of precision in dealing with the condition.

Before organized trading began the quotations for eggs of the Chicago Butter and Egg Board and the prices at which terminal egg dealers were willing to contract for eggs with egg shippers provided the best available indications of egg price levels. At that time also the prices which dealers were willing to pay for butter and eggs for refrigeration while production was seasonally in excess of consumption were basic to butter and egg prices during those periods. Of course there were price series also in major consuming centers, notably at New York.

With the rise of organized trading at Chicago the bulk of the contracts for future delivery came to be made on the Chicago Mercantile Exchange publicly under standardized procedures and for definite grades. The prominence of the November futures for butter and of the October futures for eggs tended to direct attention to the conditions likely to prevail at those times. With comparable quotations and other statistics for previous years readily available the machinery was well adapted for the determination of the best estimates of future prices on the basis of the imperfect information available at the times when the respective quotations were registered. While the value of the quotations was impaired at times by imperfections, such as manipulation in the trading machinery, the prices registered by organized trading in butter and egg futures represented a definite improvement over the previous prices.

This is not to say that further improvement was not possible. Better appraisals of future conditions by individual traders offered an opportunity for advancement. Too many traders based their operation too much on hunches or tried to follow what they thought that the trade leaders were doing instead of making reasoned estimates of demand, supply, and prices of refrigerated butter or eggs.

Organized trading also contributed to increased efficiency in price determination after the respective periods of accumulation. Daily records of futures quotations provided the best indexes of the market values of refrigerated butter or eggs. Frequently only scattered data of sales of such commodities were generally available, perhaps without definite information as to the quality represented. The information as to futures prices was available to show how the prices of the refrigerated commodity compared with those of the fresh, helping dealers to adjust their offerings to popular demand.

Organized trading promoted an improved price structure for butter and eggs by making it easier for buyers and sellers at wholesale, jobbing, and retail levels to keep in touch with the values of basic grades of those commodities. Because the great bulk of the futures contracts in both butter and eggs was traded at Chicago, the influence of the quotations there was felt throughout the surplus-producing areas. While its effect upon the price structure may have been greatest during the respective seasons of accumulation, its effect during the remainder of the marketing year for each commodity was increased by the scarcity of market prices for refrigerated butter and eggs. Thus the wide dissemination of futures quotations tended toward greater uniformity of prices of butter and eggs.

In addition, organized trading opened the way for arbitraging or spreading among butter futures and among egg futures, giving traders an opportunity to keep each of the futures in line with industry estimates of developing conditions.

Organized trading assisted in the transfer of ownership of butter and eggs by the delivery of limited quantities on futures contracts.[6] This service was more important in butter and eggs than in grain or cotton. Although nearly all speculators and most hedgers closed out their futures positions in butter and eggs by means of offsetting transaction, a number of hedgers chose to deliver part or all of their holdings on futures contracts and some jobbers and retailers preferred to accept delivery rather than to purchase from wholesalers. Cold storage warehouses or the dealers financed by such warehouses were prominent among the dealers who made delivery.

A few wholesalers, jobbers, or even retailers sometimes accepted delivery as a means of obtaining butter or eggs. Some of the smaller jobbers preferred to accept delivery of eggs rather than to purchase eggs from wholesalers, in part because by accepting delivery they were assured of grading by the Exchange inspectors. The preference of some of the smaller dealers for deliveries is interesting because ordinarily it might seem that the larger dealers would enjoy an advantage in accepting delivery since they presumably could fit the varying qualities which they might receive into their trade better than a small dealer could.

A few dealers assumed long positions early in the life of a future for the purpose of obtaining delivery comparatively early in the delivery month. Some might

[6] Much of the material presented under this heading is based upon an unpublished study by the writer, entitled "Deliveries Upon 1939-40 Chicago Egg Futures".

assume long positions late in the delivery month if it appeared that they could obtain butter or eggs to better advantage in that way than by private purchase. Thus the alternative of acceptance of delivery provided a check upon the premiums over the futures which could be obtained by dealers who were merchandising refrigerated butter or eggs.

Organized trading provided quotations suitable for wide dissemination since the quotations are simple and require comparatively little space. Thus they were particularly well adapted to transmission by telegraph, telephone, or radio and for publication in newspapers. Since the contracts were highly standardized any change in the quotations represents a change in the price level. The quotations were readily understood, once the public had become informed about them.

In contrast to the futures quotations the cash prices for a given grade frequently represent a range of prices at the same time within the grade because of variations in quality. A single cash price would require comments as to the quality of the lot sold in order to cover its implications fully. Both cash and futures prices contribute to an understanding of the market but if only a limited space is available the meaning of the futures quotations is clearer.

Organized trading furnished a continuous, convenient market for hedgers and speculators, permitting them to change their futures positions quickly if the need arose. Ordinarily, contracts could be entered into or closed out at any time within the appointed hours of the trading sessions. In this respect a futures market tends to differ from a cash commodity market which tends to vary in length of time with the quantity to be sold. If supplies on hand in a cash market are large the market may be active for a considerable period; if they are small many buyers are likely to leave after a short time and a stray lot arriving late may find only a few bidders.

Furthermore, organized trading provided the advantages of standardized contracts and trading procedures which cut down the friction ordinarily involved in transacting business.[7] Since the contracts were highly standardized they can be entered into readily and any one might be substituted for any other in the clearing process. Standardized trading procedures also greatly facilitated the trading.

The foregoing observations should not be construed, however, as an unqualified endorsement of the trading in butter and egg futures on the Chicago Mercantile Exchange. It contributed to a substantial improvement in the handling of the butter and eggs accumulated by dealers but there was room for further progress, particularly in the determination of prices. It may be observed also that the Exchange which began as a Chicago project was helpful primarily to Chicago dealers and to other dealers who stored butter and eggs at Chicago. The influence of the Exchange extended far beyond Chicago and several adjustments were needed to permit its services to keep pace with its widened responsibilities.

Value Of Organized Trading Will Depend Upon Rules Governing It

The evolution of organized trading in butter and egg futures and available information concerning such trading in other commodities show that organized trading in futures was developed to cope with definite problems in the marketing of the commodities traded. Its continued value in the marketing of butter and eggs will depend upon perception of the needs of changing marketing systems and the adoption of rules to make the trading responsive to such needs.

Two fundamental changes to which trading in butter and egg futures must adjust are (1) the sharp reduction in the consumption of butter and (2) the

[7] "Standardized contracts in and of themselves partake of the general nature of machine production. They materially ease and cheapen selling and distribution. They are easy to make, file, check, and fill . . .". (54)

shift in the seasonality of egg production. These conditions require changes in marketing practices which, in turn, call for adjustments in futures trading. Other marketing changes likewise should be reflected in organized trading in butter and egg futures if that trading is to be of maximum service to those commodities.

Opposition to that trading within the industry has been materially reduced since 1922 when certain elements in the Chicago Mercantile Exchange attempted to abolish organized trading in butter and egg futures. Few in the industry now would abolish organized trading but some in the trade as well as some producers of butter and eggs would like to do away with certain parts of it, particularly speculative short selling. Some others object to the small proportion of contracts settled by delivery and to the range of grades which may be tendered in settlement of contracts.

The opponents of speculative short selling seem to feel that large operators are able to obtain profits through depressing prices by means of heavy and concentrated short selling and then, in some mysterious way, covering their short sales at the lower price levels. These opponents would hardly assert that this can be done on a small scale — attempts have been repeatedly unsuccessful — but they have the notion that somehow clever operators can do it on a large scale. Accordingly, they would like to have short selling declared illegal.

It is true that short selling has been associated with numerous sharp declines in commodity prices. Analysis of a number of such declines, however, discloses that they followed periods of over-optimistic buying which had forced prices upward to levels from which they presently would have fallen of their own weight.[8] In such instances the short sales were not the prime

[8] For evidence on this point see (73).

cause of the declines. Short selling hastened the declines and probably accentuated them. At such times it may be very profitable. When prices are at about the level warranted by existing conditions, however, short sales are likely to be unprofitable. A market axiom is "Never sell a dull market short".

One real abuse of short selling is that when prices are declining sharply, after having been pushed to unduly high levels, the impetus of heavy short selling may drive prices below the proper level. A conspicuous instance was in wheat early in 1925 when prices dropped from more than $2.00 per bushel to below $1.40 before becoming stabilized at about $1.70 per bushel. Such effects could be largely avoided by providing that during sharp declines no speculative short sales could be made below the level of the previous quotation. This rule has been adopted by the security markets at the insistence of the Securities and Exchange Commission. Such a rule in commodity futures would eliminate the main objection to short selling while preserving its advantages.

The objection that too few deliveries are made on contracts is inconsistent with hedging which requires that most contracts shall be settled by offset rather than by delivery. At the beginning of organized trading in butter and egg futures it appears that the transfer of ownership by means of delivery was common but with the development of hedging the transfer of price risks without giving up possession of the commodity became predominant. As to the view that too many grades are tenderable on contracts, the number represented a compromise between too many grades on the one hand and the danger of manipulation on the other.

More important than the foregoing items are the various practices which tend to reduce the net services rendered by organized trading in the marketing of the commodities traded. Such practices tend to increase as an exchange grows older and its futures operations become more complex. One or more traders chance upon a method of trading which is profitable, frequently because it takes advantage of certain technical conditions in the market. Other traders learn of it and use it. One example in wheat and corn futures was the tendency for prices of an expiring future to decline relative to more distant futures in the month prior to delivery, provided that supplies for delivery were adequate. This tendency arose from the eagerness of the longs in the expiring future to close out their positions lest they be forced to accept and pay for delivery early in the delivery month. (48) (49)

The difficulties of controlling such practices increase with growth of futures trading in a given commodity. At the beginning, nearly all the members of an exchange are familiar with the marketing of that commodity and can see readily how the marketing is affected by the futures trading. As the trading grows, particularly if it comes to occupy the full attention of a number of the members, a decreasing proportion of the membership is well informed concerning both the marketing of the commodity and the organized trading. In such circumstances it becomes harder to keep the rules adjusted to the marketing needs of the commodity and to control various practices which cut down the net value of the organized trading in futures. In the absence of definite information as to the effects of various practices the attitude of many members tends to be that if a practice is profitable it must be making a contribution to the marketing of the commodity.

As the older members of the Exchange are replaced, the membership tends to divide into three main groups. At one extreme are a comparatively few members who are active in analyzing conditions and in pointing out the need for improvements. At the other extreme are some members who oppose any changes, frequently because they are getting profits from existing conditions. For example, some may hope to profit from squeezes by making trades themselves on congested markets; others may be favored by receiving commissions on some of the transactions of manipulators. Between the two extremes are ranged the remaining members, generally well-meaning and interested in promoting the efficiency of the organized trading but preoccupied with their immediate affairs. This group is not always sure of the need for changes nor of the results which would follow from the changes proposed by the reformers.

Of course members shift from one main group to another from question to question, according to their knowledge of the matter at issue, personal inclinations, financial interests, and other factors. The inertia of a large proportion of the membership favors a lag in adjusting the rules of trading to the needs of changes in marketing. In general, the group interested in promoting increased efficiency is a minority and must obtain considerable support from the large middle group in order to obtain a majority and get the changes adopted. Furthermore, vigorous enforcement is difficult in an exchange, as in any organization, if only a bare majority favors a rule.

Although such tendencies toward undesirable practices, if unchecked, would cut down the net public value of organized trading in butter and eggs futures, they can be overbalanced by vigorous action on the part of Exchange and Governmental agencies. Such action would be aided greatly by improved popular understanding of the services of organized trading in marketing the respective commodities. It should be borne in mind that a high degree of efficiency in butter and egg futures had been attained by approximately 1940. Further increases in efficiency can be attained only by careful analysis and intelligent planning.

Exchange activities are essential in promoting greater efficiency in the services rendered by organized trading to butter and egg marketing. Recognition by the leaders and a large proportion of the members of the Exchange that service to the marketing of butter and eggs is the end purpose of futures trading in those commodities will go far toward keeping down the growth of practices which will interfere with that service.

Encouraging signs include the earlier actions taken by the Exchange toward the control of "squeezes" and the innovation, adopted after a trial period in the early 1940s, of placing non-member representatives of the butter, egg, and vegetable trades on the Board of Governors, the rule-making body of the Exchange. These representatives are in a position to bring the needs of their respective industries before the Board of Governors.

Government supervision likewise will aid in promoting the efficiency of organized trading in Chicago butter and egg futures. Government activities here add to the consideration given to the interests of producers and consumers of butter and eggs. Organized trading in those, and other, commodities is placed under the supervision of the Secretary of Agriculture by the Commodity Exchange Act which renders certain practices illegal and provides for the investigations necessary to bring out the facts concerning practices operating against the public interest. Representatives of the Secretary are closely in touch with trading practices and urge constructive measures upon the exchanges.

Furthermore, the Act empowers the Secretary to make a thorough analysis of the organized trading in futures in each commodity traded. This authority has been used sparingly. Such studies could show in what ways the trading facilitates the marketing of the respective commodities and what practices, if any, cut down the value of its services.

Much could be said in favor of such studies being made by the respective exchanges for the information of their members and as a basis for publicity. Such studies, properly conducted, would give the members of the respective exchanges a much clearer picture of exchange operations and functions than is generally available to them and would strengthen the hands of the constructive minority which is interested in increasing the efficiency of the services rendered by the organized trading.

Since information developed by the various exchanges, however, might be viewed with suspicion by the public there would be good reason to have the studies conducted by a public agency. They would contribute definite information as to the changes, if any, needed to increase the value of the organized trading to the marketing of the respective commodities. The information obtained would be, likewise, of great educational value and would help to clear up many of the popular misunderstandings concerning organized trading in futures. Public sentiment concerning butter and egg futures now is much colored by current impressions concerning the long established cotton and grain futures. From the standpoint of public relations the traders in futures in each commodity have a real interest in seeing that studies are made which will bring out the services rendered by the trading in other futures as well as in their own.

Popular recognition of the ways in which organized trading in futures promotes efficiency in marketing would permit consumers, and especially producers, to concentrate on working for improvements which are practicable rather than to follow will 'o the wisps of imperfections in the trading. Per person, producers would be more interested in improvements in efficiency than would consumers, since there are fewer producers than consumers of farm products. Informed public interest in exchange efficiency would stimulate feelings of responsibility among exchange members.

A major way in which popular recognition of the marketing services rendered by organized trading would contribute to increased efficiency would be by improving the judgment of the speculators who take the other side of the hedges. This could be done by encouraging the participation of more well-qualified men and deterring that of unqualified traders. Under present conditions the opposite is true. A number of well-informed men who are shrewd judges of the price levels warranted by existing conditions do not enter the futures markets for fear of social disapproval, including the stigma of gambling. In contrast, some traders enter the futures markets without analysis of market conditions and with no more thought of responsibility for the price level of the commodity than they would have in placing a bet at the race track. Popular realization of the part which speculators should play in arriving at the best estimates of future prices would help to reverse this situation and thus would help to reduce price fluctuations.

Considerable improvement in the popular understanding of organized trading in butter and egg futures as well as of that in other commodities may confidently be expected to result from the analysis of futures trading which is being conducted by the Brookings Institution. While the report upon this analysis is not yet available, sufficient evidence is at hand to indicate that it will brush aside some misconceptions which were based on partial information and provide an adequate explanation of the marketing services rendered by organized trading in futures. Additional improvement also may be expected from the studies of marketing conducted under the Research and Marketing Act of 1946, provided that these studies include accumulation of inventories by dealers and processors. Better understanding of the problems of accumulation would aid in appreciating the assistance provided by organized trading in handling those problems.

APPENDIX I.

DEVELOPMENTS IN GRAIN AND COTTON FUTURES WERE SIMILAR

The foregoing material shows clearly that the time contracts and the organized trading in butter and egg futures which succeeded them arose primarily from the efforts of dealers to cope with the problems resulting from accumulation of butter and eggs. Detailed examination of time contracts in grain preceding the beginning of organized trading in grain futures at Chicago reveals generally similar developments. In cotton futures the available evidence indicates a similar pattern of evolution.

In both grain and cotton the beginning of organized trading in futures was preceded by about 20-25 years of time contracts. In grain, time contracts in corn at Chicago were reported in 1851; in cotton, time contracts attracted attention in New York in the same year. In both grain and cotton the evidence points to considerable evolution in the time contracts before they ripened into organized futures trading. After the transition to organized trading was effected, the organized trading in each showed a great deal of development before it became full-fledged. In both grain and cotton there is reason to believe that the developments in time contracts and in organized futures trading were in response to the needs of a rapidly growing commodity market.

Time Contracts In Corn Arose Early At Chicago

Because the marketing of grain at Chicago at the opening of the Illinois and Michigan Canal in 1848 differed greatly from present conditions it may be helpful to sketch the background. There were no railroads at Chicago and all movements of grain into, or from, the city were by wagon or boat. Much of the grain arrived in farmers' wagons or sleighs although

Plank Roads Were More Important Than
Railroads to the Chicago of 1850

large quantities also were sent in by wagon by interior merchants who purchased grain from farmer customers or accepted it in trade. Nearly all the grain shipped from Chicago went by boat and large quantities frequently were stored in the city during the fall and winter, pending the opening of navigation on the Great Lakes in the spring.

Transportation was expensive. About 1844, when wheat prices were low, it appeared that the value of wheat was about equal to the cost of hauling it 60 miles. (64) Some wheat was teamed much more than 60 miles to Chicago in a number of years, however, according to reports. Corn was of less value per bushel than wheat and could not be hauled profitably as long distances as could wheat. With the exception of one year when corn was shipped to Ireland to alleviate the effects of the potato famine there, the arrivals of corn at Chicago before 1848 were only slightly in excess of local requirements.

The opening of the Canal in April, 1848 resulted in a great increase in the corn business at Chicago. Farmers responded promptly to the presence of a cash market for corn along the Canal and the Illinois River. The increase is indicated by the data of shipments of corn from Chicago for the five years 1847-1851. The figures are: (3)

1847	67,315	bushels
1848	550,460	
1849	644,848	
1850	1,262,013	
1851	3,221,317	

Trade comments indicate that the 1850 shipments were reduced by the near failure of the corn crop in the South in 1849 which caused relatively high prices for corn at St. Louis and drew corn away from Chicago. (8)

Dealers invested heavily in facilities to handle the increased quantities of corn. By January, 1851 numerous corn cribs had sprung up along the Canal and the Illinois River. Some of the cribs were large and substantial stocks of corn were accumulating in them. (16) Reports of heavy movement to the cribs continued throughout the winter and by March 5 it was estimated that about 2,000,000 bushels of corn had been accumulated between Chicago and St. Louis. (17)

Probably most of the corn was hauled to dealers' cribs during the winter. Roads were primitive and might be nearly bottomless after the spring break-up. Corn could be hauled conveniently by sleigh. Even if there were not enough snow for sleighing, the roads were solid when frozen.

Dealers needed to hold corn in the cribs to permit it to dry thoroughly before shelling and shipping. Some of the early shipments in 1848 and other years spoiled on their long journey by water. (14) Most of the corn did not reach Chicago until the summer. Average monthly percentages of receipts of corn at Chicago for the five years 1854-1858 were:

January	0.6	May	11.1	September	15.0
February	1.0	June	17.3	October	7.2
March	2.2	July	18.5	November	3.0
April	5.7	August	17.8	December	0.6

Very likely the proportions were much the same in the previous years.

Obviously the erection of cribs, the installing of shellers, and the financing of the stocks of corn must have strained the resources of many country corn dealers. No information was obtained as to the extent to which corn was purchased outright by the dealers in early days. In some instances such dealers may not have set a price upon the corn until they had been able to sell it, but doubtless competition among dealers for corn operated powerfully toward purchase by the dealers. In the mid-1840s some Chicago warehouses advertised that liberal advances would be made upon grain and other farm products accepted for storage. Very likely some local dealers found it necessary, at least to make advances, and perhaps to purchase the corn outright. Probably the proportion purchased tended to increase as the business grew.

Even though a dealer might be making money the need for new capital to expand his operations could well continue pressing. Usually, he would desire to expand at least as rapidly as his competitors and he would be unwilling to turn away the farmers in his trade territory when they desired to sell corn lest he lose them permanently as customers.

In such circumstances it is not surprising that some dealers should enter into time contracts with Chicago buyers. The general practice was thus described by a former member of the Board of Trade:

> "In the early days when the canal was constructed, men wanted to buy corn, crib it in the country, and hold it till spring when the canal opened. They used to come to Chicago and hunt around for some man who would buy the corn for May; then the commission man would advance the money for the corn. This enabled the man living in the country to buy the corn of the

farmers, crib it, and hold it until navigation opened . . .". (1)

The first time contract found in Chicago grain market reports as part of a continuing process was in corn on March 13, 1851. It called for the delivery of 3,000 bushels of corn in June at a price 1 cent per bushel under the quotation for corn that day. (18) Four days later, other contracts calling for the delivery of corn in June were reported, quantities not stated. On April 18, when the Canal was under repair, the market report read in part, "Considerable doing in corn and we note sales of 10,000 bushels, deliverable after the opening of the canal . . ." (20) On May 3 contracts for 10,000 bushels of corn afloat were noted at 30 cents per bushel, to be delivered between the 15th and the 25th of June. (21)

It is recognized that earlier contracts forming a continuous series may have been made but not reported in the market reports of the daily paper where the contracts noted above were found. Isolated references to earlier contracts were found. In 1845 a market comment was, "We learn that one large lot (of wheat) changed hands, deliverable in the spring . . .". (10) Four days later a Buffalo dispatch stated that a New York dealer was willing to contract for wheat for spring delivery. These reports, however, seemed to be isolated. Another contract in October, 1850, when corn was 40-42 cents per bushel, called for the delivery of 30,000 bushels of corn the following June at 28 cents per bushel. (15)

Time contracts in corn continued in 1852 but were not mentioned in as great detail as in 1851. Late in February a weekly review noted, ". . . But little has been done in corn for present delivery, owing to the bareness of the market. Contracts for future delivery have been sparingly made at about 45 cents, half cash." (11)

In 1852, also, time contracts in wheat were noted in Chicago market reports in that paper. On March 2 a contract for 10,000 bushels of spring wheat for delivery on board vessel between April 1 and 15, payment on delivery was reported. On March 6 the same paper mentioned several contracts for wheat to be delivered at the opening of navigation. In one the terms "cash"; in another they were "half cash". On March 10 several time contracts for the delivery of wheat in April were reported.

Why did the time contracts in wheat appear later than those in corn although wheat marketing developed first? Presumably because the problems of accumulation were less acute in wheat than in corn in the early 1850s. Shipments of wheat from Chicago fell off from the 1848 and 1849 levels and did not equal the 1848 shipments for four years; in fact, for the years 1850-56 inclusive shipments of corn exceeded those of wheat. While an interior trade in wheat was developing in the Chicago area, it does not appear that interior wheat buyers had as pressing problems of storage, financing, and risk assumption as did corn buyers.

The Cash Corn Market in 1856

It is true that frequently large quantities of wheat were accumulated at Chicago before the opening of navigation on the Great Lakes, especially when most wheat was teamed to the city. The spread of the railroads west of Chicago, beginning in 1850, changed the situation so rapidly that by 1855 it was estimated that only about 3 percent of the receipts of wheat came by team but before 1850 nearly all of it was teamed. With favorable weather large quantities of wheat could be teamed to Chicago after harvest before the close of navigation but a wet autumn would cut down the movement and would tend to increase the quantity held in Chicago. Wheat could be hauled more conveniently by sleigh during the winter than it could be transported by wagon for some time after the spring "break-up" of the prairie roads. This and other factors contributed to sizeable stocks of wheat at Chicago before the opening of navigation.

Stocks of wheat at Chicago about March 1, 1846 were estimated by the Chicago Journal at 682,000 bushels. About half was owned by Eastern interests, about a tenth by farmers, and the remainder by Chicago dealers. As interior grain buyers made their appearance, they doubtless held part of such stocks at Chicago. Market comments from time to time noted that part of the arrivals was being stored for the account of the shippers. Some of the warehouses arranged for advances on the grain stored and very likely it was easier to finance the grain held in a Chicago warehouse than the corn held in a dealer's crib in the country.

Railroad shipments of wheat and corn eastward from Chicago exerted little influence upon the early development of time contracts in those grains. Not until about the beginning of 1853 was rail communication opened from Toledo. Even by 1855 only about 1 percent of the corn shipped from Chicago went by rail and while nearly 10 percent of the wheat shipped went by rail that proportion included short hauls to mills in nearby States.

It appears that the time contracts in corn and in wheat were considered as distinct from the sales made "to arrive" which ordinarily referred to grain shipped or about to be shipped. "To arrive" sales of corn were mentioned in market reports almost immediately after the opening of the Illinois and Michigan Canal in April, 1848. No time limits were noted in any of the early "to arrive" reports, perhaps because it was expected that the corn would be brought in as quickly as practicable. After the time contracts had been reported they did not displace the "to arrive" sales which continued to be mentioned. Both contracts contained an element of futurity but in the "to arrive" contracts it related primarily to the uncertainly of the time required in shipment; in the time contracts to the time when shipment would be made.

Time contracts were employed also in pork packing which then was a highly seasonal business. In April, 1851 it was noted that, "Contracts have been entered into for pork to be delivered at Terre Haute next fall at $3.50 per 100 lbs." (19) It appears also that contracting in advance for the delivery of hogs at specific prices had become common at Cincinnati by 1851. (62)

Use of time contracts in grain marketing in the Mid-West increased rapidly but irregularly during the 1850s. Their use was greatly stimulated by the activity in the grain trade which resulted from the Crimean War. In December, 1855 it was reported that, ". . . the corn which was expected to pass this port by June 15 had probably all changed hands once or twice by prospective contracts. . . .". The following year, however, the same observer noted that there was little disposition to look forward. (12) Very likely the lack of aggresiveness in 1856 represented the customary let-down after a period of great activity.

Time contracts were employed extensively in grain marketing in other cities, particularly at New York, by approximately 1855. It is possible that their use in some of the older grain markets may have begun earlier than at Chicago.

After 1856 it appears that the use of time contracts

Two Chicago Terminal Elevators of 1860

in grain marketing increased at a moderate rate for several years. (4) They then received a great stimulus from the activity in the grain trade which resulted from the Civil War. Their growth and development continued until they ripened into organized trading in grain futures, perhaps early in the 1870s.

This finding as to the beginnings of grain futures at Chicago differs from the account given in Taylor's "History Of The Board of Trade" which attributes them to "arrive" contracts. That statement reads:

> ". . . The trade in futures began in a perfectly natural way. The storage capacity of Chicago was limited. It frequently happened that a northeast wind brought in a large fleet of vessels when there was little grain at Chicago, but plenty of corn and oats in storehouses along the line of the Canal or Illinois River, and in later years along the railroads. Under these circumstances it was a convenience to the vessel owner, and to the Chicago grain merchant as well, if some holder of grain in the country, or some Chicago agent of such country owner, would agree to deliver it in Chicago within a specified time, i.e., 'to arrive within 5 days' or "to arrive within 10 days'. . .". (65)

The account is plausible and has been generally accepted in the absence of evidence to the contrary. It would be inferred that the "to arrive" contracts developed at Chicago because of the conditions noted. Such contracts, however, were in use at Buffalo in 1842-43. (13) Probably they were extended to Chicago as soon as there was use for them there. It does not appear that they were related directly to grain futures.

Time Contracts Showed Evolution

While little direct evidence is at hand concerning the early time contracts in corn and wheat, it is reasonable to conclude that they were informal and in keeping with the crude nature of early grain marketing. Only the quantity, price, and time of delivery were specified in the early time contracts reported although in some the proportion of the price paid in cash was given. They may have been verbal contracts although a memorandum may have been kept by both parties. The contracts were personal and each party relied principally upon the integrity of the other for fulfillment of the contract.

In a few years some of the contracts, at least, were written. Doubtless a number of them were drawn with a view to making them enforceable at law. A written contract for the sale of corn was the subject of a lawsuit in Stark Circuit Court (Illinois) in April, 1852. (53) Another lawsuit, Porter v. Viets, showed that,

> "... On the third of April, 1857, ... Viets entered into a contract in writing with the plaintiffs, by which he sold to them 15,000 bushels of corn at 48 cents a bushel, delivered free on board during the last half of June, and both parties executed the contract. ..." (61)

Nothing was stated as to quality of the grain in the reports of the early contracts. Here it should be borne in mind that time contracts arose several years before the Chicago Board of Trade first established grades for grains in 1856. Presumably the contracts in the Chicago territory after that time tended to provide for Board of Trade grades, including the developments in those grades.

Although the evolution of time contracts in grain marketing cannot be traced in detail from the material at hand, it is known that well before organized trading in grain futures began a high degree of standardization in the time contracts had been attained. Units were in thousands of bushels, contracts were generally standardized in written form, most of the trading was for delivery in specified calendar months, and the contracts had lost much of their personal nature and passed from hand to hand.

Control By Board Of Trade Began In 1865

As was to be the case about half a century later in the Chicago Butter and Egg Board, the leaders of the

Chicago Board of Trade were slow to extend official recognition to the developing time contracts. One view was, ". . . The conservative men who controlled

> affairs at the time, however, seemed to think there was too much of the element of chance in this method of trade. . . ". (66)

Another partial explanation may be that the strongly financed firms who were influential in the Board tended to look askance at the traders with limited capital who were active in the trading in time contracts.

It should be borne in mind that the Board of Trade had comparatively little influence up to about 1856 and that it developed very rapidly in the next few years. Organized in 1848 on a general basis, it struggled for existence for several years and among other things it attempted to stimulate attendance by offering a free lunch to members. In 1856 it gave evidence of increased vitality by adopting grades and standards for grain. In 1858 the first call was made for the restriction of the business transacted on the exchange to members of the Board. A charter dated March 7, 1859 was obtained from the State of Illinois. Among other provisions it conferred broad powers upon the Board's Committee of Arbitration and Committee of Appeals and authorized the Board to appoint inspectors, etc., whose certificates should be binding upon the membership. Obviously, there were many matters to occupy the attention of the leaders of the Board.

The first rule of the Board dealing specifically with time contracts was adopted in May, 1865. It provided for the deposit of margins on time contracts, not to exceed 10 percent of the value of the commodity specified in the contracts, on the demand of either party. This rule was much like the first one adopted in connection with time contracts by the Chicago Butter and Egg Board about 45 years later, approximately

10 years before the beginning of organized trading in butter and egg futures.

The 1865 rule of the Board of Trade, however, had been preceded by one applying to all contracts which had been adopted March 27, 1863. It read:

> "Any member of this association making contracts, either written or verbal, and failing to comply with the terms of such contract shall, upon representation of an aggrieved member to the Board of Directors, accompanied by satisfactory evidence of the facts, be suspended by them from all privileges of membership in the Association until such contract is equitably or satisfactorily arranged and settled. And it shall be the duty of the Board of Directors to cause to be publicly announced to the Association the suspension or restoration of any member suspended under this rule." (2)

From the adoption of the 1865 rule it may be inferred that the effects of the 1863 rule were inadequate with respect to time contracts.

When the General Rules of the Board of Trade were adopted on October 13, 1865 the May, 1865 rule on time contracts was incorporated in them. At that time, two other rules dealing with time contracts were adopted, one setting forth the procedure to be followed in the event of failure to deliver and the other providing some standardization of delivery upon time contracts and method of payment.

These initial rules of 1865 concerning time contracts on the Chicago Board of Trade presently were followed by others from time to time as the Board extended its control over the trading in time contracts. Evidently there was resistance on the part of the more conservative grain handlers to the increasing use of time contracts and probably a great deal of inertia had to be overcome before adequate rules could be obtained. Furthermore, the supporters of time contracts, and of organized trading, were blazing trails in unexplored territory and could deal with new conditions only as they developed.

It appears that the transition from trading in time contracts to organized trading in grain futures was effected gradually. Without a detailed study of the rules involved and their enforcement it is difficult to determine the time of the transition but perhaps a fair estimate would be between 1870 and 1875.

Organized Trading Underwent Evolution.

Available evidence indicates that organized trading in grain futures developed greatly from comparatively crude and simple beginnings in the early 1870s. One element in its evolution was the rise of hedging to reduce price risks on an accumulation of a commodity while retaining possession of the commodity for merchandising or processing. Evidently hedging of grain did not become common for some time following the beginning of organized trading in grain futures. Basing his opinion largely on practices described in a lawsuit and in testimony before a committee of the New York Senate about 1883, Hoffman suggests that hedging of corn on the part of country grain dealers became common some time in the 1870s and that the hedging of wheat was common in 1880. (46) An earlier observer, however, asserted that about 1876 everyone trading in wheat futures at Chicago preferred the buying side with the result that futures were high relative to cash wheat. (45) Some color is given this assertion by a reported conversation between Mr. Pillsbury of Pillsbury Mills and Mr. F. H. Peavy who had built up the great line elevator company. Mr. Pillsbury recounted in 1898 that some years previously Mr. Peavy had told him that all he had to do was to fill up his houses with wheat, sell "May" as a hedge, and he was assured of several cents a bushel profit. Mr. Pillsbury replied that the day would come when that practice would not be possible, for no business was assured of a profit without effort. (See 47).

Futures prices more than a carrying charge higher than cash grain prices do not suggest that hedging was widespread. On this basis it appears that hedging in wheat futures may not have become general until a little after 1880.

More information concerning the development of speculation also would be helpful in appraising the development of organized trading. Speculators in grain from outside the grain trade appeared at Chicago at times in the 1840s, according to market reports, and there is reason to believe that for a considerable period there were numerous "investment buyers" who bought wheat after harvest in anticipation of an advance in price later in the season. Such buyers purchased physical wheat and either stored it or arranged for its storage. Presumably some such buyers dealt through brokers in their purchases and subsequent sales, substantially as was the case in butter and eggs before organized trading in butter and egg futures. (See pp. 28-9) With the development of the system of grain warehousing, speculation in grain tended to shift to warehouse receipts, facilitating speculation by persons outside the grain business. Then the development of organized trading in grain futures provided a more convenient and economical means of speculation in grain. The convenience of speculation (and hedging) was increased by the rise of futures commission merchants with numerous offices to solicit business. It is possible that much of the earlier opposition at interior points to organized trading in grain futures, ostensibly on other grounds, traced to local brokers and dealers who had lost the business of their "investment buyers".

Development Of Cotton Futures Was Generally Similar

The evolution of time contracts and organized trading in cotton futures resembles closely that of grain or of butter and eggs in its broad aspects. Although less detailed information is presented concerning it, the pattern of the rise and development of time contracts in cotton, the inauguration of organized futures trading, and the further development of that trading are clearly apparent.

Because the cotton trade in the United States was closely connected with that of England over a period long before the beginning of organized trading in cotton futures, it was to be expected that cotton marketing developments in one country would be reflected in the other. Accordingly, it is convenient to consider the time contracts and the organized trading in cotton futures in both countries.

Time contracts were reported in New York in 1851, nearly 20 years before the organization of the New York Cotton Exchange. (34) At Liverpool, time contracts were mentioned as early as about 1857 and their volume increased greatly during the Civil War in the United States. (35) (44) While a detailed analysis of the evolution of time contracts in cotton was not attempted, the limited evidence conveniently available points to considerable development of these contracts before they ripened into organized trading in cotton futures. Writing in 1925, Cox suggested about 1860 as the time of the origin of trading in future contracts although he was careful to state that professional speculation in cotton had begun earlier, in Liverpool in the early part of the 18th century. He noted also that

> ". . . The contracts for forward delivery of cotton soon came to be traded in from one buyer to another, probably passing through several hands before the time for actual delivery. The increased negotiability made necessary the uniform usage of terms in the contract and uniform methods of settlement. Moreover, they were no longer made to cover specific shipments and were filled from any cotton available." (25)

Organized trading in cotton futures at New York evidently began early in the 1870s. The New York Cotton Exchange was formed on a voluntary basis as an association of merchants and brokers in the summer of 1870 and received a charter from the State of New York, passed April 8, 1871. Writing in 1872, Donnell commented that the business was entirely new and almost every rule was experimental. (32)

The 1872 rules of the Exchange indicate organized trading in futures. They provided for a standardized contract with margins to be deposited and maintained at the request of either party to the contract, for transfer or cancellation of contracts, for definite grades deliverable on contracts, and for standardized procedure in delivery and in payments. In addition, a number of other rules governed various phases of the trading.

Presumably organized trading in cotton futures at New Orleans began a little later than at New York. The New Orleans Cotton Exchange was organized in 1871 but trading in time contracts on it was not active for nearly a decade. (5) (6)

Organized trading in cotton futures at Liverpool probably began later than at New York. This is suggested by Dumbell who indicated that action could be taken more promptly at New York becaues it was not a great spot market for cotton, nor was it bound by a thick accretion of custom as was Liverpool. His observation is in accord with the scanty information readily available on this point. While the Liverpool Brokers Association adopted certain regulations in 1869 dealing with time contracts the first provision for margin deposits was made in 1871. (36) Very likely the transition from time contracts to organized trading in cotton futures at Liverpool occurred gradually a few years after 1871.

There is reason to believe that organized trading in cotton futures, like that in grain and in butter and eggs, developed to a considerable extent after its beginning. Hedging presumably made its appearance some time following the inception of organized trading, finally becoming widespread and highly important to cotton marketing. Speculation developed also, being powerfully affected by hedging requirements and by the convenience and economy of speculating in futures rather than in actual cotton or even in warehouse receipts. It is reasonable to conclude that other functions of organized trading in cotton futures also developed gradually in response to market needs and that the organized trading was of much greater service in the marketing of cotton after 20 years of development than at its beginning.

Additional research in the development of grain and cotton futures might well disclose other points of resemblance to the development of butter and egg futures. For example, Dumbell relates that a concerted attack upon the 'objectionable gambling practices' of time contracts in cotton was launched by merchants and spinners at Liverpool in 1870. "The attack was

> directed against contracts for future delivery . . . on the ground that little or no capital was required and that people who had nothing to lose were induced to engage in them. The critics gained one point at least, namely a common agreement to make mutual deposits. The agreement was voluntary in 1870 but was formally recognized by the Cotton Brokers' Association's rules in 1871. . .". (36)

This opposition in cotton was much like the opposition to organized trading in butter and egg futures in 1922 (p. 42).

The evidence presented, however, is believed adequate to warrant the conclusion that trading in grain and cotton futures reveals the same general pattern in development as did butter and egg futures approximately half a century later, both in the unorganized and in the organized form. The degree of correspondence between the development of grain futures and of cotton futures was too close for co-incidence but no indications were found that the futures trading in either grain or cotton influenced that in the other. The most reasonable explanation of the similarity in development is that in each commodity it was in response to generally similar changes in marketing conditions and to similar needs.

Such a conclusion is consistent with the similar pattern of development shown by butter and egg futures roughly fifty years later which was shown to result principally from developments in butter and egg marketing, especially from the accumulation of butter and eggs by wholesale dealers. In each instance the pattern was much the same. First came the rise of time contracts. Then there was a period of development of those contracts in various ways and finally the time contracts matured into the early stages of organized trading in futures. Following that there was a period of development in the organized trading, in hedging, in speculation, and in other elements, largely in response to the growth of the respective commodity markets in size and complexity, until the organized trading attained comparative maturity.

APPENDIX II.

EGGS IN COLD STORAGE ON JULY 1, 1896 AND 1895

From: New York Produce Review II:17, July 16, 1896

"Late in June New York Produce Review sent letters of inquiry to a large number of correspondents in all sections of the country where storage facilities for eggs were known to be located, asking for estimates of the quantity of limed and refrigerator eggs put away in the various localities, compared with the quantity held last year on July 1.

"The letters were addressed to public cold storage houses and to egg merchants, and of the total number addressed a very large proportion returned estimates or positive statements." This was the first attempt of this paper . . . .

"We have secured more than one estimate in most of the larger centers; where these have been at variance we have taken the most reliable whenever we have had opportunity to judge; otherwise we have tabled the average of the estimates."

The result of the investigation is tabulated as follows:

	1896	1895
NEW YORK STATE		
New York City	115,000	130,000
Nine other reports including Buffalo, Little Falls, and Syracuse	114,500	71,700
NEW JERSEY		
One report	50,000	30,000
PENNSYLVANIA		
Philadelphia	110,000	125,000
Five other reports including So. Bethlehem, Pittsburgh, Pottstown, and Reading	108,097	127,926

MASSACHUSETTS		
Boston	77,300	90,500
Two other cities	23,000	10,000
RHODE ISLAND		
One report	36,000	48,000
CONNECTICUT		
Average of two reports, one city	37,500	42,500
OHIO		
Thirteen reports, including Cleveland, Tiffin, and Cincinnati	102,850	117,310
INDIANA		
Three reports	5,000	6,500
ILLINOIS		
Chicago (average of reports)	335,000	370,000
Four other reports, including Elgin	34,300	30,100
MICHIGAN		
Seventeen reports, including Detroit, Richmond, and Williamston	30,400	39,400
MINNESOTA		
Seven reports including Minneapolis and St. Paul	44,800	24,400
IOWA		
Thirteen reports, including Sioux City, Des Moines, Burlington, Waterloo, and Nevada	164,550	199,800
WISCONSIN		
Nine reports, including Reedsburg, Johnson's Creek, and Richland Center	29,900	27,900
MISSOURI		
Two reports	14,800	15,000
KANSAS		
Five reports	4,500	4,700
NEBRASKA		
Four reports including Omaha, Hastings, and Lincoln	15,400	17,300

SCATTERING

One report each from W. Va., La., Tenn., and D. C.	6,650	6,150
Total	1,495,547	1,534,186

LITERATURE CITED

(1) Allerton, S. W.
FICTITIOUS DEALINGS IN AGRICULTURAL PRODUCTS: 173. Hearings, Committee on Agriculture, House of Representatives, 1892

(2) Andreas, A. T.
HISTORY OF CHICAGO: 361

(3)
Ibid.: 556

(4) 1859
ANNUAL REPORT OF THE CHICAGO BOARD OF TRADE: 8-9

(5) Boyle, James E.
COTTON AND THE NEW ORLEANS COTTON EXCHANGE: 70 (1934)

(6)
Ibid.: 100

(7)
Bulletin 101, Bureau of Statistics, United States Department of Agriculture

(8) 1853
Chicago: HER COMMERCE AND HER RAILROADS: 5. Chicago Democratic Press

(9) 1922
CHICAGO DAIRY PRODUCE: 1. December 26

(10) 1845
CHICAGO DEMOCRAT, THE. December 5, 9. Ibid. December 31

(11) 1852
CHICAGO DEMOCRATIC PRESS, THE. February 23. Ibid, February 23.

(12) 1856
Ibid. December 31
(13) 1843
CHICAGO EXPRESS, THE. January 30
(14) 1849
CHICAGO JOURNAL, THE. June 30
(15) 1850
Ibid. October 18
(16) 1851
Ibid. January 24
(17)
Ibid. March 5
(18)
Ibid. March 13
(19)
Ibid. April 16
(20)
Ibid. April 18
(21)
Ibid. May 3
1894
CHICAGO PRODUCE:
(22)
Ibid.: 12 November 17
(23)
Ibid.: 1 December 22
(24) 1896
Ibid.: 4 June 20
(25) Cox, A. B.
EVOLUTION OF COTTON MARKETING: 17. 1925. Processed. Bureau of Agricultural Economics, United States Department of Agriculture
(26) 1878
DAILY COMMERCIAL BULLETIN, Chicago December 30
(27) 1879
Ibid. December 19

(28) 1881
Ibid. January 6
(29) 1884
Ibid. April 18
(30) 1874
DAILY COMMERCIAL REPORT AND MARKET BULLETIN, Chicago. May 20
(31) 1877
DAILY COMMERCIAL REPORT AND MARKET REVIEW, Chicago. November 27
(32) Donnell, E. J.
CHRONOLOGICAL AND STATISTICAL HISTORY OF COTTON: 614 (1872)
(33) Duddy, E. A.
COLD STORAGE INDUSTRY IN THE UNITED STATES, THE: 4. (1929)
(34) Dumbell, Stanley
ORIGIN OF COTTON FUTURES. Economic History I: 259
(35)
Ibid.: 261
(36)
Ibid.: 265
(37) 1895
EGG REPORTER, THE: 5. April 15
(38)
Ibid.: 15, April 15
(39)
Ibid.: 23, May 15
(40)
Ibid.: 4, June 15
(41) 1896
Ibid.: 11, May 20
(42) 1899
Ibid.: 23, May 20
(43) 1900
Ibid.: April 7
(44) Ellison, Thomas

COTTON TRADE OF GREAT BRITAIN: 274 R. Wilson, London, 1896

(45) Hammesfahr, F.
CORN TRADE AND OPTIONS MARKET, THE: 14 Antwerp, 1899

(46) Hoffman, G. Wright
FUTURE TRADING ON ORGANIZED COMMODITY MARKETS: 377. (1931)

(47)
HEDGING BY DEALING IN GRAIN FUTURES: 78 University of Pennsylvania Press

(48) Hoffman, G. Wright
TRADING IN CORN FUTURES: 19-20. Technical Bulletin 199, United States Department of Agriculture

(49) Irwin, H. S.
SEASONAL TENDENCIES IN WHEAT FUTURES PRICES. Processed. January, 1936. Grain Futures Administration, United States Department of Agriculture

(50)
SURVEY OF EGG FUTURES. Processed. September, 1940. Commodity Exchange Administration, United States Department of Agriculture

(51)
SURVEY OF BUTTER FUTURES. Processed. March, 1940. Commodity Exchange Administration, United States Department of Agriculture

(52) Kunkel, . . . (N. Y.)
HEARINGS HELD BEFORE THE SELECT COMMITTEE OF THE UNITED STATES SENATE RELATIVE TO WAGES AND PRICES OF COMMODITIES: I:635 April 12, 1910

(53) 1858
LAW v. FORBES. 18 Illinois 568

(54) Llewellyn, K. L.
CONTRACT. Encyclopedia of Social Sciences

(55) Marsh, A. R.
REGULATION OF COTTON EXCHANGES: 225 Hearings, Committee of Agriculture, House of Representatives, 1914

(56) 1898
NEW YORK PRODUCE REVIEW AND AMERICAN CREAMERY: 28. April 19

(57) Ibid.: 21. September 28

(58) Ibid.: 668, March 11, 1903

(59) Nourse, E. G.
CHICAGO PRODUCE MARKET, THE: 38. (1918) Houghton Mifflin Company

(60)
Ibid.: 39

(61) 1857
PORTER v. VIETS' I Bissell 177

(62) 1852
REVIEW OF THE TRADE AND COMMERCE OF CINCINNATI: 5. Cincinnati Chamber of Commerce

(63) 1911
RULES OF THE CHICAGO BUTTER AND EGG BOARD: 12

(64) Taylor, Charles H.
HISTORY OF THE BOARD OF TRADE OF THE CITY OF CHICAGO: 121. (1917). Robert O. Law Co.

(65)
Ibid.: 193

(66)
Ibid.: 317

(67)
Ibid.: 649

(68)
Ibid.: 710

(69) Thompson, C. W.
STUDIES IN EGG MARKETING: 10. Bulletin 132, Minnesota Agricultural Experiment Station, April, 1913

(70) 1924
United States Department of Agriculture, YEARBOOK: 385-6

(71) Wiest, Edward
BUTTER INDUSTRY IN THE UNITED STATES, THE: 168. Columbia University Press, 1916

(72) Working, Holbrook
WHEAT FUTURES PRICES AND TRADING AT LIVERPOOL SINCE 1886. Wheat Studies XV:137-8. Food Research Institute, Stanford University, California, November, 1938.

(73)
CYCLES IN WHEAT PRICES: Wheat Studies VIII. Food Research Institute, Stanford University, California, November 1931.